SWEPT AWAY

a story of survival

Dale Chimenti

Email Address: dalechimenti@yahoo.com

dalechimenti@gmail.com

Cover design by The BrainWerks

DEDICATION

*To my children Stefanie and Joey
who bring me pride and joy.*

*In loving memory of
Carl and Gloria Chimenti,
who shall forever live in my heart.*

CONTENTS

A C K N O W L E D G E M E N T S

My friend, Spencer L. Ballard, D.O. who has ministered to my every ache, physically and emotionally, for many years. I am thankful for his breadth of knowledge on a very wide range of topics. I am a beneficiary of his many years of formal education and his innate intelligence. My thanks to Spence for all the quirky nights we spent together editing this book.

My lifelong friend, Jim Hric, who has given much more than he has received, and who always worries about me.

The game of handball. It has been my therapy.

My fraternity of handball friends who have accepted me as one of their own. In particular, Jim Golden, a real handball champion and athlete, for his patience and generosity.

For those of you I missed, you know who you are.

INTRODUCTION

The following memoir has come to life as a result of the persistent efforts of my wife, Liz, who feels that I have something significant to say in the aftermath of my journey at sea. I have always felt that my thoughts are my own with little or no value to others. An incredible experience it has been. A compelling story? Without a doubt.

I struggle in the body of this work to find the words to describe the emotional experience of being lost at sea. I share the dialogue of my thoughts as I remember them, but suspect that I cannot possibly color these pages with a literal expression of the feelings that coursed through my mind as they occurred. If I have missed the mark in sharing the deep psychological touchstones buried within this experience it is only that I lack the skills or aptitude to intellectualize and therefore, articulate, that which may be obvious to others better educated than myself. The reader is left to paint a picture of this story and feel its impact as a "personal experience," with reliance on each individuals' own fears and anxieties; for the true "telling" of this story lies in the emotions that reside, singularly, in the minds of each of us. This writer and this story act only as a catalyst in awakening the most positive expectations and the worst fears in all of us.

I also found myself writing this story for everyone else, concerning myself with grammar and sentence structure in the hope that my skills as a writer would make for compelling reading. In the process I discovered my limitations as a writer, grew to hate the work, and finally, broke free of all that nonsense with the realization that my experience was truly incredible— all by itself. With the facts forever branded in my mind, and the wisdom of our friend, and sometime attorney, Dean Bruza, who, early on, had the foresight to record a lengthy video histography, my work became a simple matter of factual input.

It is, then, a work in progress, a collection of thoughts in the aggregate. In the absence of any extraordinary intelligence or profound wisdom, I give you the story of a man....

SWEPT AWAY

IN THE BEGINNING

Archangel Guyayon most likely never imagined he could sing like an angel, but that he did when he yelled "man overboard," tossed the ring, and completely ruined the actuarial tables. They say life begins after death. Certainly this was the case on that summer in winter day somewhere in the middle of the Gulf of Mexico. The M.S. Almania, port of registry Hamburg, Germany was steaming out of Progresso, Mexico toward its final destination of Port Everglades, Florida. By any standard, a behemoth totaling 308' of solid steel, carrying its daily pay of containerized cargo both refrigerated and otherwise, in its belly; also a day late, 10 degrees off its normal course, and unaware that it would soon have a passenger. In conventional parlance, by the grace of God and all the powers of the universe converging in the same place at the same time, all for the purpose of saving one sure to be dead sonofabitch.

Three days and interminable nights is a long time to swim alone only to be interrupted with the appearance of a ship. Besides, I had already seen a ship earlier that day and it was much prettier, radiant white and alluring, coaxing me with an irresistible power and offering passage to another place in the universe. That ship interrupted a journey that seemed to have started a long time ago; In the next moment, or perhaps hours, gone, as inexplicable as its arrival. Passage revoked. For now, however, the journey and this story begins much earlier.

A friend of mine always talked about how I "live large" and how he hoped to become successful and live like me. I found that term reasonably amusing, particularly since I considered my lifestyle and spending habits conservative. But I understood his point of view. On the ladder of life, he was about 3' away from the ladder and I at least had both feet on a few rungs, one above the other.

Since I was a kid, I had been hustling for money; a variety of paper routes, shoveling snow, bagging groceries- I was always working. I loved that buck and chased it with enthusiasm. I went into business early on. Having survived the good years and the bad, but mostly good, it was business as usual in the winter of 1994 when my wife and I decided to take our two children on a well deserved vacation.

We included my Godson Danny Carcone in our plans. Danny worked at my restaurant equipment company as a parts administrator, serviceman, computer geek, all around do anything that needed to be done kind of guy; as long as it didn't interfere with eating or getting laid.

Danny and I have been co-conspirators in wacky and immature behavior. We raced our go-kart at excessive speeds in the parking lots surrounding our building, weaving in and out with reckless abandon, just to beat the stopwatch. Danny and I even challenged each other to a boxing match. What started as a harmless challenge to don boxing gloves turned into a full scale event. One of our employees built a regulation size ring in his backyard, invited guests, handpicked 3 judges, and we were on. We fought 7 three minute rounds. It turned into a brawl. I was fighting like Joe Frazier, well not really, but I was covering up like him, and Danny lost his temper. I wouldn't give him a target and he was really angry. We beat the crap out of each other. He came within an inch of knocking me out in round 3, but I hung in there and won the decision as well as a small purse collected from all the fight fans. He got two black eyes. It was beautiful.

Danny is the product of a broken marriage with a twist. His parents, both well educated, chose to remain persona non grata within the confines of their family home. Danny's father, a wacko, chose me to become his son's spiritual soldier. Of course, his father had to be a wacko to select me as his son's Godfather. His mother, in her benevolent ignorance, simply didn't know better. Nonetheless, at the primordial age of 16, I became THE GUY in Danny's life. The very sober nature of that appointment was not lost on me, however. Despite my age, I felt the weight of responsibility squarely resting on my shoulders. Danny's spiritual development became my responsibility and I was ready. It is now some 29 years later, seems like yesterday morning, and I still feel like I'm the band leader.

It was Danny's fault! It was Danny who said "lets go jet skiing down in Cozumel." It was Danny who went down to the beach in front of the hotel on the morning after our late night arrival and announced that he had found the rental shack! I was a reluctant but willing participant. How could I let him know that the prospect of putting my toes in that ocean terrified me. No way. In actuality, there is no one to fault for the sequence of events that subsequently unfolded; just another experience in the conundrum of life.

You know, I still haven't seen Cozumel from land. My recollection of the island is so compressed. We arrived in the evening after spending considerable time at the airport in Cancun awaiting a flight to take us the short distance from the mainland to Cozumel.

Danny and I decided to go out and have a few cocktails. We walked along the main thoroughfare while deciding which bar to begin our evening of revelry. Danny needed to refine his skills at hitting on women, so he selected a woman who had to be at least 15 years his senior. I admired his guts. Here stood a woman who clearly would not consider him a candidate for anything more than a loan for the purchase of an ice cream cone, and he's going for it. As suspected, his efforts were for naught; but he anticipated the refusal and it didn't phase him a bit. My boy! He was truly a predator. Afraid of nothing. No Willy Loman here. Couldn't sell her? Ok...later. Time to move on. I envied his freedom to schmooze the women.

We finally made it to the bar and Danny's salacious inquiries began in earnest. He found some babe to dance with and I had just about enough. It's painful to watch him dance. He really should be embarrassed. People with no bladder control need Depends. Danny can't control his arms and legs and should be in a straight jacket...I took a cab back to the hotel.

THE   JOURNEY   BEGINS

It wasn't a great view, but awakening to azure skies with the promise of tropical heat was simply paradise. There is something richly textured and tangible about tropical climes for those of us accustomed to the harsh forces of the North American winter. My wife, Liz, and our two children, Stefanie age 9 and Joey age 6, couldn't wait to begin their day. We decided to go down to the pool and lay claim to our very own lounge chairs. Seasoned pool dwellers, we knew the ground rules. Get chairs early, plant flag, and to hell with the rest of the poor slobs who don't have the foresight to stake an early claim.

It was only a few minutes after settling in did Danny appear, much like Kramer exploding into Jerry Seinfeld's apartment, to declare that he had found the jet-ski shack. We were going. NOW. 55 bucks each. Cash. I'll never forget the fear I felt, walking up to that thatched roof hut. I immediately sensed that Jet-Skiing was a distant stepchild to the wide variety of scuba and deep sea fishing activities offered. A thick glossy binder with the smudged prints of a thousand hands flipping through page after page of available charter vessels perched upon the bar.

Talking to Danny and myself is not an easy thing to do. We
love chaos. Anyone encountering the two of us at the same time is
in for an interesting exchange. We are the yin and yang of mouth.
We don't shut up and we don't budge an inch until we are satisfied
that we have driven our subject to exhaustion or lifted any personal items on their person including jewelry, wallets, and pens.
Danny and I practice the art of pickpocketing. Just for fun, but very
slick and we always return the merchandise. Except for pens. We
treat pens as exempt from "Thou Shalt Not Steal." After all, life is
fraught with peril. Caveat Emptor. Lose your pen? Too bad for you.
Pay attention. We could have kept the cash.

Such was the mind set as we approached the diminutive
young Hispanic man with the toothy grin. —And he thought we
were the garden variety American touristas. We sure showed
him...much later that is.

Having paid in cash for the hour long rental, the rental agent
demanded that we produce a credit card as a security deposit for
the return of the Jet Ski's. Danny and I looked at each other,
emitted bellicose grins, and asked the guy, "what are you talking
about? We are in the middle of two oceans on an island owned by
a foreign country, and we're not going to return these Jet Skis?????"
He insisted. We complied. An ominous tone that set into motion
a series of events that would irrevocably change the course of my
life. The laughs were over.

As we stepped away from the rental shack, having concluded
the transaction, it finally hit me that we were definitely going out
into that very scary water. I would never admit it, but as a 10 year

old kid, wearing sneakers while swimming in Michigan's inland lakes was high on my wish list. Were it not for the fact that I would be forever branded a sissy, having all the fish removed was a pretty good idea too.

How was it that no-one else had fears like mine? I can't imagine Danny having anxiety about wading out into the ocean and hopping aboard a jet-ski. He looked at me as we gazed at the rocky shoreline being slapped by the hard foamy water and said, "You go first." Hmmn. He must be testing me, I thought. "There is no room for equivocation here." Hell, if I hesitated even a second, he would sense it and I would be in danger of destroying my reputation as a bad ass. This is "WAY TOO TOUGH DALE" we are talking about, a moniker given me by an old acquaintance, Chico, a few years earlier, and evidenced by a key ring emblazoned with the acronym WTTD etched upon its surface, and alluded to enthusiastically whenever possible.

Yep, I was going first.

I waited at the waters edge while my jet-ski was being serviced in the water adjacent to the dock. Danny pointed to a faded and tattered life jacket hanging from a piling and suggested, pointedly, that I should put it on. The only direction we had received from the rental agent was to stay away from the cruise ships and with a casual flip of the hand extended above his head, to "stay in front of the hotel" and not go down toward the other hotels.

The idea of a life jacket did not strike me as significant, despite my fears. I knew that jet-skis were virtually unsinkable. Danny's insistence that I wear a life jacket would figure prominently as the pivotal ingredient in keeping me alive long enough to strive for some new goals in my life.

Having earlier shed my half inch wide, Italian gold bracelet with a typical dago-tough guy-bad ass "hang on to this babe, I'll be back-I got some business-fahgedabowdit" admonishment to my wife, here stood a DIFFERENT kind of guy now removing his glasses, folding one stem over the other, gingerly placing them on the counter of the rental shack AND NOT FEELING REAL STRONG about walking into the ocean.

I waded into the water alone, half blind, and barefoot. Shoes would have been very nice. Before me, a landscape of jagged rocks for a pair of feet whose only crisis heretofore, was wearing rubber vs. leather; tenderfoot would have been an understatement. The water was very cold, the environment uncomfortably foreign to me.

I stood in waist high water patiently waiting for the attendant to wind up his attention to my jet-ski. He appeared to experience some difficulty in preparing the machine for departure. There was no warning flag in my mind. I was, by reputation a sharp businessman. Yea right, how many times had I made foolish choices or been conned into believing something that was simply not so—and there was no warning signal?

The mechanic wiped his hands on a greasy shop towel, placed the towel in the rear of the machine and motioned for me to come over and hop aboard the starboard side while he started the engine again. He asked me if I had ever ridden a jet-ski. I responded negatively, whereupon he proceeded to point out the location of the throttle. I noticed a black wrist band with a C shaped clip attached to one end and inquired as to its purpose. He offered that the clip with its attendant wrist band was a kill switch in the event the rider was thrown from the machine, the idea being that if the rider was thrown from the machine the engine would quit.

I had no intention of testing that theory. No sirreee. I would not become separated from the jet-ski. I had absolutely no plans to engage in behavior that would lead to being thrown into the ocean—vast, dark, cold, and alive with monsters of the deep.

"What the hell," I pressed the throttle down with my right thumb and headed out to sea, hoping Danny was right behind me. "Come on Danny, get your ass out here so I'm not alone." There was no panic, but this was not Lake MiniHaha.

It wasn't long before Danny caught up with me. Now we were going to have fun. I followed his lead in riding to the crest of a wave and jumping over. "Hey, this is fun!" The jet ski was very responsive to the slightest pressure on the throttle. I squeezed the handgrips powerfully and muscled the jet-ski from one swell to another. We weaved in and out of each others path and headed out for deeper water and hopefully, even larger waves. We estimated that the further from shore, the more turbulent the water. This was not particularly the result— but we were satisfied that we were having fun. The speed was thrilling enough. When we became bored, we pulled to within a close but safe distance from each other to talk and take a break. Danny and I both remarked how beautiful a day it truly was. Clear, bright blue skies, a hot yellow sun unencumbered by clouds, and a moderate breeze. It would be the last peaceful moment in my life. Those beautiful blue skies and moderate breeze would become a beast of burden. WAY TOO TOUGH DALE was about to find out just how tough he was.

I T ' S   A   B E A U T I F U L   D A Y

It stalled and wouldn't restart. "How could this be?" Danny's machine kept running as we sat idly. I wondered what could be wrong. Danny glanced at me with that "you are clueless" look, convinced that I had flooded the engine or committed some other foolish error, certain that I was truly one of the uninitiated in the fraternity of allknowingness. I had always trusted Danny's instincts in the line of fire. Never shy and always an aggressive stance in the face of difficulty, he quickly warned me to suspend my efforts to start the jet-ski fearing that the battery would wear down. No passing motorists out here. Danny suggested that we trade machines and he would try to start mine.

His attempts to start my jet-ski failed. Kawasaki pieceajunkski was dead in the water. Well, maybe the battery would restore itself if given a brief rest. We returned to our respective machines.

How it is that both Danny and I, in our not insubstantial collective experience did not see the signs of trouble will forever remain a mystery to me. In all the years in business, all the years Danny worked for me, —in all the businesses I can recall and more I probably can't remember, we had been lied to, cheated, robbed, embezzled, conned, hustled, had our buildings torched by fire, been broken down on the road a long way from home...countless other experiences. Where were our instincts? What went wrong? Were we overconfident? Ignorant? Did we blatantly disregard the potential dangers?

As I reflect upon that day, it is clear that nothing in our lives prepared either of us for the decisions needed at that moment; nor was I prepared for the consequences of those decisions. The dynamics of those decisions, the point of origin, must have been a function of my experience in business; handle the little problems quickly and don't sweat the big stuff. Perceive of a problem as being big and surely it will grow even bigger. Ignore it, and the passage of time will undoubtedly alter its course.

Controlling interest in our adventure shifted back to me when after a short restoration period the jet-ski was deemed to be hopelessly silent. We had dismissed the possibility of towing the craft due to the size of the waves and the absence of rope. Locking hands was out of the question. It was at that moment that I made a decision that will forever haunt me.

"It's a beautiful day. I'm going to lay back on this thing and get a tan. You go back to the hotel and get some help. I'll be right here when you get back." "Are you sure?" he shot back at me. "Yea, man we're not that far out. I can see the hotel from here. Just be quick."

As he turned his jet-ski toward shore, I recalled the old nautical adage about never leaving your buddy. Squinting at his back in the bright glare of the sun, I was struck by the realization that

I had just made the mistake of my life. In the span of just a few moments Danny disappeared from sight. I couldn't even see where he had gone. He had vanished. I knew I was going to die.

Like the child who drops the glass and is struck with the irreversible course of events born at the moment the glass shatters into a thousand pieces, I too felt the weight of helplessness. Not the anticipation of parental discipline as in the fate of the child; rather, the instant revocation of my license to live. I specifically recall saying to myself, "Dale, you are in big trouble. You have been in trouble before, but you are really in trouble this time." This was different. These were real bad odds.

"I don't want to be out here alone. NO. NO. NO. Some ship could run over me. Sharks. There are sharks out here."

Not more than 15 minutes had passed when I began to seriously consider taking affirmative steps to save my life. There in the near distance sat a cruise ship anchored in place and presumably filled to capacity with vacationers. Despite the death sentence I had talked myself into, I was hesitant to solicit their attention. Above all else there is the matter of dignity. I would be embarrassed to seek help; besides Danny was getting help. They were bound to arrive soon. "And how would I board that big monster anyway? All those people looking at me derisively, laughing and pointing at the drunken fool. Anyway, how would I get to shore? Oh, what a mess."

In the next breath I cast those concerns about dignity aside as survival became first priority. "What can I do to save myself right now?" I had to get the attention of someone on that cruise

ship. Sitting astride the large leather and foam seat (with an 8"
split on its top seam) which served as a cover for the engine, I
shifted my bare feet to the center of the channels which ran down
each side of the seat, and stood up. "I can't see anyone, but I
don't have my glasses on and they MUST be there." I didn't hear
any sounds. No laughter or sounds of merriment. I postulated
that I must be out of hearing range, but within sight. After all, I
could see the ship. Therefore, "they must see me. I'm not waving
my arms for fun. I'm out here, you're in there, hah, hah. "Oh
look honey, see the man waving at us? Lets be friendly. Wave back!"

The specter of not being taken seriously suddenly became a
minor concern for without warning, the jet-ski became, at once,
unstable beneath my feet. All my efforts to regain balance were
futile and I was abruptly thrown into the water.

The machine had completely flipped over. "Oh my God,
I'm in the water. I don't want to be in this water, and this thing is
upside down. Try to get it righted. Look, there are slots in the
bottom center. Put your fingers in there and pull." Too heavy. It
wouldn't budge. "All right, hoist yourself up onto the top with
your legs in the water, balance your torso with your belly, reach
up over the opposite side and pull up again." Having done so, the
jet-ski popped up and was once again in the floating position for
which it was designed. "Thank God for small miracles."

"Lets go again. Get onto the machine. Sit down. Steady. Settle
in. Hold the handlebars and give it a minute. What's with the
gurgling sound? Is this thing taking on water? Never mind. Get
your ass up and start waving again." Even more carefully this time,

I rose from the seat only to be dumped, unceremoniously, into the water once again.

It became apparent, after righting the craft once more, that it had taken on a tremendous amount of water. I could not understand how this could come to pass. Jet-skis are to grownups what plastic boats are to kids in the bathtub. Dunk 'em and they pop right back up, ready to go again. This indeed was not the case. I could no longer attempt to stand up and wave for help. I would have to be satisfied with sitting and waiting; not a popular option for a man of action.

Survival, like life itself, was a constant succession of adjustments. Waiting would be tough but I could do it.

———— I was not going to be so fortunate. I scrambled onto the machine again, only to discover, with horror, that it would no longer support my weight. I could no longer board the machine. No sitting. No standing. I WAS IN THE WATER FOR GOOD.

"Why am I not seasick?" I speculated that one has to be in a boat to feel the effects of motion sickness. I did not experience any nausea normally associated with the pitch and roll of the ocean. I wasn't seasick, but suddenly began to violently retch. This primitive physiologic reaction to fear was a cruel hoax being perpetrated by my body that would quickly deplete badly needed bodily fluids. It was also dangerous and stupid and an immature reaction to fear.

I shaped up quickly. "No more throwing up, Dale. You may need whatever fluids are in your body. You could be out here a while. Stop tossing NOW. Hold it down." —and hold it down I did. I had not eaten any food since the prior day so my stomach was empty anyway. I mentally shifted the fear from a physiologic reaction to a focus on survival. A clear cold transition from vulnerability to a rational work ethic began to emerge.

I decided to stay with the Jet-ski. That decision having been made, it was time to settle into a routine and find the most comfortable way to await the posse'. I placed my elbows onto the two channels at the rear and with arms from the elbows up to the hand in a position parallel to my body, I held onto the rear of the seat. Without the weight of my body, the jet-ski at least allowed me to keep my upper arms and head out of the water. It was uncomfortable but I felt a modicum of security having something to hold onto.

Considered only in the brief time I could see land, I had never seriously pondered swimming to shore. With land no longer in sight, I brooded the wisdom of that decision. —I was many, many miles out by then. I was very concerned that a boat might not see me or the jet-ski but decided that I would be considerably more visible by partnering with "this useless piece of junk."

Within the first few hours several opportunities for rescue passed me by. I yelled and waved at a hydro-foil passing by with a full load of passengers certain that someone would see me. With all the people aboard I couldn't imagine that not a single pair of eyes would not cross my position. But none did. Before long a passenger jet lumbered into the air in a slow laborious effort to gain altitude. I was convinced that it was flying the short little route between Cancun and Cozumel, and had just taken off as it passed over me. "Come on, dip your wings. Let me know that you see me." To this day, despite the fact that I should know better, I'm convinced that pilot was looking the other way or not at all. That jet was SO close.

Suddenly, the sound of an approaching boat jolted me to full consciousness. I must have been daydreaming, or dozing. "How long have I been here?" The familiar sound of the outboard transported me back to the summer of '65. Cass Lake; Uncle Bill's house; Uncle Bill telling us kids the story of the swimmer who wandered past the buoys and was chopped in two by a speedboat. Fun with an asterisk. That lake was forever changed in my eyes. No longer innocent; a friend no longer.

The green boat became louder as I struggled to shake the lethargy that had a grip on me. "Dale, how could you be so lazy? Why didn't you hear it sooner? You are reacting too slowly. There it is! Wake up! It's turning away from you," and I said to myself," I am tired. Another boat will come. Don't worry."

With those words I began the long, lonely journey into the center of the Gulf of Mexico.

I ' M   H E R E   F E L L A S

It really didn't feel odd striking up a conversation with the sharks. Hey, if we never engaged in dialogue with the big bear, the former Soviet Union, we may have experienced World War III. From where I sat, dialogue was good. There were no other alternatives. Sharks strike indiscriminately, at will, and I knew there was an abundance of marine life around the island of Cozumel. Located approximately 40 miles east of the Mexican mainland, its southern end touching the northern tip of the Caribbean, its northern shore at the southernmost waters of the Gulf of Mexico, it is common knowledge that scuba divers from around the globe visit Cozumel to experience some of the most beautiful coral reefs in the world. The food chain is in attendance in vast numbers. At the top of that chain are the big guys, sharks. I knew that I would have to deal with them.

A psychologist later suggested that I suffer from a severe case of post traumatic stress disorder and cited the following conversation with the sharks to support her opinion. Maybe she had something there. Then again, maybe all she had was my $85.00

I looked out into the open waters and at the perceived audience directly in front of me and said "Fellas, I'm here and I know I'm in your backyard and I'm here to tell ya that you have NOTH-ING to fear from me," remembering the opening scene from Jaws where an unsuspecting girl swimming in the ocean was stalked by a shark. The camera, as if it were the eyes of the shark, cut through the water from below the surface as the girl kicked and thrashed about. The shark moved closer and closer until...

With this in mind, I spoke out loud to the sharks, "I have places to go. I know that you know that I am aware that you are here and I DO NOT FEAR YOU. Do not fear me. I will not splash around like the girl in Jaws, but I MUST SWIM. I will be moving my arms and legs in a determined manner. You will not detect any fear."

I never felt as much control over my life as I did in that moment. I believed that I could influence the actions of the sharks through my subconscious thoughts and beliefs, and vocalizing them. I knew that the sharks would not hurt me. As a practical matter, were I attacked, death would come quickly. The process of eliminating fear on both the conscious as well as subconscious level was a matter of examining the process of death. First, a shark attack would not be a long tortuous event. Besides, I would not feel sorry for myself. Victims of the holocaust suffered years of torture and death. "You do not qualify for sympathy. You must be a man and deal with this," I told myself.

I assumed that a first bite would sever at the minimum, a leg and therefore a major artery culminating in death within seconds. Mercifully, I would probably lose consciousness within that time frame. In a body that had lived for 40 years, I could tolerate 60 seconds of pain. I then examined the nature of that pain. I envisioned as most likely, being cut in two just above my hips in one precise pass. No anger on the part of the shark. No menace. Just business. Sharks doing just what sharks do. I would feel a very brief, hot, searing separation of my body into two pieces, the lower portion of my body torn from the upper trunk and disappearing into the depths. My eyes would look down, not in horror, but in recognition of my final moments. Death would follow very, very quickly. The only negative consequence of that death would be that my family would never know what happened. They would not have closure. At that moment, thoughts of death were of no value and simply negative, for in order to save my life it was necessary to examine the concept of fear and remove it. To that end, I waved to the sharks and continued on, resolving never to fear sharks again. They sensed my strength. We had a deal. Powerful stuff. In the aftermath of this incredible experience, there is little I give myself credit for, but I am quietly and privately, very proud of myself and in awe of the power of the human mind in the matter of the sharks. Sadly, however, to this day, I still find myself, inexplicably, in tears all too often.

M I D - A F T E R N O O N   D A Y   1

Sharks aside, it was time to re-assess the situation. First I would take stock of my worldly possessions. Inventory did not take long. I owned one purple bathing suit and one yellow gold ring with a .95 carat diamond. My mother would be proud of me. I'm sure she would have preferred I own a Chris Craft in the instant, but hey, at least I had good taste. At any rate, I sure didn't have extra baggage. It occurred to me that I needn't concern myself with being naked and that my well being would be better served by removing the bathing suit from my ass and placing it over my head for protection from the elements. It turned out to be one of my better plans. My plan did have one major flaw, however. I was not concerned with the ring glistening in the water and attracting predators because I had long since decided that my presence would be of surprise to no one. Every fish in the ocean knew I was there. Wander into any backyard with a dog in residence and it'll be friend or foe in short order. What concerned me was the delicate state of the flagship. Male ego notwithstanding, exposing myself to any number of interested parties could be big trouble. "What if something bit me?" An innocent nibble would spell disaster. The ring may not draw attention, but I feared my most important appendage would draw attention. Contrary to the humorous nature of that problem, slow death was a certain consequence of being bit. Not only would I bleed to death, but the first scent of blood and my deal with the sharks was over.

I began to cling, tenaciously, to the idea of surviving this ordeal whole and completely intact. I was not prepared to sacrifice anything. I would emerge in one piece or not at all. I concluded that if I were bit on my penis or toes or anywhere else, I would be fair game and die anyway. The anatomical particulars didn't matter. Naked it would be.

I placed the bathing suit onto my head with the elastic waist band forming a tight fit across my forehead over and past my ears and completing the circle by winding around the back of my head just above the neck. The waistband afforded me the best protection from the constant crashing of water into my ears. It kept me sane.

Spitting. "Dale, you are spitting way too much." Every few minutes I felt the need to expel the salt water from my mouth. Another in a long list of decisions, each with a contrary and equally relevant solution. In the matter of spit vs. no spit, which course of action was the right one? Drinking salt water will bring on sure death. "If I do not expel the salt water, I will eventually swallow enough to soak my internal organs to the point of complete shut down. On the other hand, if I continue to spit, my saliva will piggyback on the salt water as I purge my mouth and I will surely dehydrate to death. Damn. Nothing is ever easy." In the end I decided that I would retain the salt laden saliva and try to keep my mouth closed. I could probably live longer by not dehydrating.

Now, every thought was punctuated with a reminder of how thirsty I was, and the value of every drop of water I could retain.

A   G E O G R A P H Y   L E S S O N

Land was no longer in sight. In its wake I was left with an overwhelming sense of dread, a horrifying contrast to the bold posture
that I had demonstrated earlier. So much for confidence and
power; a constant roller coaster of emotions, and now the lowest
of lows. "How do I keep my wits about me when this is getting
more dangerous by the minute?"

I tried to construct a mental navigational chart and estimated
that our Hotel was situated just north of the center of the island
on its eastern shore. The island of Cozumel is 7 miles long and 4
miles wide. It never occurred to me in all the days that I spent
swimming that I was completely wrong. To this day I remain in
awe of the outcome of my journey at sea given that circumstance.
The fact is, our Hotel was located on the Western side of the island in the Channel of Cozumel. As I gazed at the Hotels in the
distance, before they disappeared from sight forever, I was looking to the East. I squinted at the sun and determined that I would
swim toward the sun as it was late in the day and the sun was
therefore settling in the west. Swimming to the west would guarantee that sooner or later I would run into the island, or at the

very least, the Mexican mainland somewhere south of the longitudinal line from where I began. They say Belize is very nice.

I was actually drifting north of the Caribbean and the channel into the bowels of the Gulf of Mexico.

My feet were so cold. My contract with the sharks and friends remained in force, but chum is a great temptation to sharks and I was beginning to feel like bait. Toes become soft and wrinkly in the bathtub. I couldn't imagine what kind of shape the flesh on my feet was in and envisioned my feet a sitting target for any of a wide variety of species cruising by. The problem was the manner of death. I just didn't want to go slowly, victim of an occasional minor bite over an extended period of time. I hoped that the end would be swift and merciful. There would be no trace of my existence. No need for a casket or urn; perhaps a photograph on an easel.

Darkness on Day 1 approached. I have never felt a more oppressive and inescapable depression as I considered the future of my children. To this day I remain sad over what could have been... "My poor children. I'm going to leave them." Most disturbing for a child's mind being the circumstances of my disappearance from their world. I would exit as a phantom that drifted away into a vast improbable void; leaving them fatherless.

There was never a question of Liz's ability to rise above the circumstances following my death. She had always been resourceful, adaptable and in control. I had no doubt she would make another life for herself and the children. She would find a way to help the children understand. She was young and attractive and quite capable of sustaining her lifestyle in a manner consistent

with that which we had become accustomed to in our years of
marriage. Our home, although modest, was entirely ours. We
owned two very successfull lingerie stores. American Freezer, Inc.
would die with me, but it had provided well. We owned a Real
Estate Development Company with my father and with fortuitous
good sense and a contribution from my mother and father, had
invested in mutual funds for the children's college education. I
was proud of my accomplishments, had made more money than
most of my friends, and never cheated anyone along the way. I
was satisfied that I had conducted my life with dignity and toler-
ance and the story of my life would be recounted without need
for embellishment or alteration. There wasn't much more that I
needed or wanted to do with my life. At one time or another, I
enjoyed nice clothes, cars, the love of a beautiful woman, a swimming pool, a good stereo... and my last vacation.

My father, mother, Liz and myself had a good laugh some 6
months after our return from Mexico. I had long ago learned
from My Father, the practice of organizing a checklist of assets
and a plan of action prior to our respective departures on vacation, in the event that we became ill, injured, hurt or worse while
travelling. It became so automatic that I had forgotten that I prepared a paper trail. I couldn't find the key to the safety deposit
box and chastised myself for losing it. Sometime later, I had occasion to be rummaging through my safe when I stumbled upon an
envelope. Inside that envelope was the key and a letter to my father with instructions on how to proceed to the next location.
Partly a simple mental exercise but more specifically, a method of

assuring a secure route to our important documents and valuables, each directive must have been completed in order to proceed to the next set of instructions. The first step was preceded by a verbal instruction to access a certain file cabinet. The final step included a key to the safety deposit box and the name of a sympathetic bank official who would allow access without interference, in the event of my demise. Gallows humor for sure, but the last sentence contained the following words: "Dad, if you are reading this letter, I am history. Not to worry, I had a great time. Have fun. Spend it. Love, Sonny." If the truth be known, my father did not find it the least bit amusing.

Returning to my ordeal in the ocean, it is still day one but the sun has gone down completely and I am in the lengthening arms of darkness. There is no doubt that any attempt to locate me would be suspended for the night. At least with daylight, the prospects of sighting a rescue ship on the horizon, however dim, was within the realm of possibility. With darkness there was no hope. For a brief time the sun and the moon shared the same sky. I knew it was important to maintain position and not lose orientation. With the visible sun the transition from light to darkness was made easier as I committed the position of the moon to memory. It was important to establish perspective for the position of the moon in the sky once the sun disappeared, so I memorized the location of the big and little dipper. With this in mind I began the journey into night reasonably confident that I could begin the next day with some idea of my location. I could not become passive. It was my job to assist with a rescue effort as aggressively as possible.

I was comforted by the conviction that Liz would have airplanes in the sky in the morning. "If I can just hang on until then, I know she will stop at nothing. She will get everybody pissed off but I know there will be airplanes in the air for me and I will be quickly located, taken to safety and this will be all over, just a nightmare from which I will escape in the morning."

"Liz, don't worry about me. I will make it until they find me. I'll be okay." With those words I said goodnight. I knew she wouldn't sleep that night. How could she? How could anyone deal with the circumstance of ones companion disappearing into the ocean? There was never a doubt that my wife faced a much more horrifying immediate future than I. I would surely die but she would face a life wondering what really happened to her husband. At that moment, floating in the darkness, I could only contemplate the depth of her pain and revisit the worst of all possibilities and the horror of which I am constantly reminded of to the present day, that I would no longer participate in the lives of my children.

Night descended as the canopy of darkness was pierced by the dazzling brilliance of a billion stars. I was immersed in a celestial light show; the only ticket holder in a theater of magnificent loneliness and desolation.

There was no one in the world on that night who had this kind of view.

I snapped out of my reverie to the uncomfortable reality of hanging off the back of the jet ski. "I need to rest for the night and continue kicking and pushing toward land in the morning. I'm not going to get any rest this way. Oh, my arms are so tired. I need to find a more comfortable position." I needed to find some way to rest or even sleep without losing my hold on the Jet Ski while sleeping and becoming separated from the machine. I needed a different position. I was so fatigued from being in the same uncomfortable position for so long. I estimated the time as approximately 9:00 PM. I had been in the water for at least 10 hours. "If I can stretch out on my back I will be so much more comfortable." I paddled to the side of the jet ski and lashed myself to the handlebar on the starboard side with the wrist band. I brought my feet up so that my toes were visible and tried to rest my back up against the side of the machine. It was my expectation that I could stretch out on my back and, with the buoyant nature of salt water, maintain a reasonably stable posture and get some sleep. Tied to the handlebar, I could set aside my anxiety over being washed away from the machine.

Well, that didn't work either. I was so damn mad. "Nothing works." The strain of the wristband against the handlegrip forced the grip to slip off the end of the handlebar and into the water. The grip was the only means of support for the wrist band. I felt like Captain Ahab in Moby Dick. Lashed to the handlebar with my back crushed against the body of the whale, waves crashing over me as the machine dove in and out of the water as I screamed out in anger. Unthrottled white hot rage. I was powerless and out of control physically and emotionally.

Although the water temperature remained constant, with the loss of sunlight I became increasingly cold. I never felt that the drop in temperature was a life and death issue; it was nonetheless very cold and became another factor in the race to maintain physical integrity while awaiting rescue. I figured that I was racing the clock. While very tired at the end of that first day, I felt very strong physically and sensed that my internal systems had a full reserve. I was also very thirsty but my immediate goal of staying alive until morning suppressed any lingering doubts over the matter of my next taste of water. I remembered an episode of Magnum P.I. where Thomas Magnum fell asleep on his surfboard and was swept out to sea. I seemed to recall that he was lost for a few days before rescue and he survived without water. I hoped that the writers were somewhat factual in establishing realistic parameters for survival in their storytelling.

Much to my surprise I spotted what I assumed to be a cruise ship off in the distance, miles and miles away. Although I could not make out any definite form, it was very colorful and I assumed land was nowhere to be seen. Swimming to the lights was not possible. It was a world away. I could only hope to be around in the morning. I have since learned that this alleged ship was most likely the tip of the Yucatan Peninsula and the last terra firma before the open waters of the Gulf of Mexico. Indeed, for me, the last proof of human existence for quite some time.

The only shelter from the elements was the bathing suit that rested atop my head and it occurred to me that I could shield my face from the night by pulling the suit completely down over my face. It wasn't necessary to scan for a rescue ship as it was dark and I wouldn't be able to see anything anyway. "If I can hunker down with my head inside, I might be able to get some sleep." As a practical matter, the fabric of the suit was soaking wet, colder against my face than the night air, and extremely uncomfortable. It was at that moment that I devised what I consider to be one of the most effective lifesaving plans I ever thought of.

Every mens bathing suit has a liner sewn into the inside. Most often a simple netting, this particular suit was made with a liner made of a tight cotton weave and in this circumstance capable of absorbing water and acting as a shield once saturated. A PERFECT TENT. I desperately craved warmth and protection from the night both physically and mentally. "If I could only make a tent within the confines of the bathing suit, perhaps I can generate some heat from my breath and at least keep my face warm." With those thoughts I put into effect a plan which on a subsequent night would save my life. I placed my hands flat on both sides of my nose on the outside of the fabric liner of my trunks and lifted the liner away from my face creating a small tent, my own private breathing space. It worked. I breathed into that little space and I was now camping out for the night. I was so happy. I was triumphant. It represented a small victory, physically. Emotionally, the "tent" was final proof that my efforts could make a difference and my spirits rose accordingly. With my cheeks warm, and an occasional shot of warmth from peeing, I was ready to conquer the night. My dad, coining a literal translation of the

Latin phrase "illigitemus non carborundum," commonly used by doctors and lawyers, always told me, "Don't let the bastards wear you down." They wouldn't wear me down that night.

H O P E   I S   L O S T - D A Y   2

Morning was a long time coming. I began the new day cold and shivering. Hour after hour of exposure to the oceans chill had left my abdomen constricted and fatigued from hours of clenching. My legs were cramped from being held in the same position for so long. My armpits continued to chafe from the constant friction and the splits in the lifevest. Hour after hour of misery

... and then at my back, where I expected it after a night of facing west, was the first glimmer of sunlight. I couldn't believe it. I had actually made it to morning. I estimated the time as 6:30 AM and I was alive to see the day. It wasn't time to break out the champagne, but this was certainly a milestone. Looking about, the scenery had not changed. I had no realistic expectation of sighting land, or seeing a rescue party, but a miracle would have been nice.

No such luck.

I knew this would be the day that "Liz will have airplanes out looking for me. It is much too early for a search party but I know they will be here later this morning." It was daybreak, time to start kicking and pushing west. They'll be here around 10:00 or 11:00."

Late morning and not a sound in the sky. "At the very least, I should be able to hear airplanes in the area even if they can't see me. Why can't I hear anything? Perhaps those lousy bastards are going the wrong way. Maybe Danny gave them the wrong directions. Are those idiots not going far enough or are they just plain stupid?" Not for even a moment did I question whether Liz had hired airplanes to search for me. I knew she would do that. There would be airplanes out there and they would find me.

The airplanes never came. They never came. I will never understand why they could not find me, but the reality was that they would not find me.

The sun was nearly straight up as morning gave way to early afternoon. Hanging off the back of the jet ski like the Ancient Mariners albatross, I continued to paddle with my feet and try to push the jet ski forward but I was going nowhere. Paddle push, paddle push. I wanted to let go but feared that I would not be seen. The same old story. I was so fatigued I was losing my ability to think clearly, and my body was losing its elasticity. My arms and legs had become unbearably heavy and incapable of reacting to instructions from my mind. My mind and body were becoming two separate entities. My groin muscles screamed at me for relief but I could not lift my leg to stretch out the groin, so I reached down, grasped my foot, and carefully pulled my leg up as far as possible. I needed relief. I could not allow any one ailment to get out of control.

Fatigue began to envelop me like a death shroud stiffening my muscles, clouding my thoughts, and separating my mind from its connections to my body.

"There has been no rescue team, or if there is, they cannot find me. This is my second day and no sign of life but my own." I had last attempted to start the jet-ski over 24 hours earlier. I decided to try one last time. I wasn't the least bit surprised that my attempt to restart the machine was futile. Even if the battery had re-charged, the engine compartment was completely submerged.

I stared blankly at my black wrist band. At that moment it represented nothing more than a grave marker. It felt like a cadaver tag. At least my remains would be identifiable by the band, so if my body is somehow found or washes up on shore my family will have closure. "My poor wonderful wife and children, I'm sorry but I am doing all that I can. Danny must be overcome with guilt. Don't worry about it Danny, this is not your fault. Liz will understand that it was Dale just being Dale, always the big boss telling everyone what to do and how to act. She won't be angry with you, she will understand." As I processed these concerns about my fate and the reactions of my loved ones I began to change my mindset. Fear was no longer pervasive. I was beginning to see that this was all about control. I had done my best up to this point to consciously identify the variables in my tiny universe and make them work in my favor. Suddenly, I experienced a willingness to address my only true enemy in all of this, which was fear. Except for a variety of physical discomforts my only concern had to be dealing with my fear. Now that I knew his identity, my enemy, I had to get inside of myself. I began to explore my feelings and expectations in the abstract.

Fear had become a mere concept as I was not in the grip of fear any longer. What was there to fear? Were my values changing or was my mind just going? Was this a strategy to preserve what remained of my life? No, I believed then as now that it was a cold, detached indifference to the fate of death. Apathy. This was the first sign of rescue - not in the conventional sense; more realistically, a rescue from the fear of dying. That death was literally on the horizon was a given. These thoughts were merely touchstones of comfort peacefully ushering life into death. Actually? It was funny as hell. I laughed and yelled out loud with enthusiasm. I was energized. "You lousy bastards, this is HILARIOUS."

Then there was the matter of the jet-ski. Perhaps letting go was not a matter of reducing my visibility from the sky, rather a reluctance to shed the last vestige of my link to life. The jet-ski was my albatross. It had brought me into this place. It had betrayed me and yet I clung to it. It was becoming obvious that the jet-ski had to go. I had held on to the back of that useless machine for one full day and had gotten nowhere.

It was time to test that hypothesis. I let go of the jet-ski and swam away from it. I took a few strokes and tried to determine whether I would accomplish anything by letting go, to see if I could actually make headway. I let go on the starboard side. Always the starboard side. Never on the other side. I don't even know what the other side of a boat is called. The other side of the jet-ski seemed forbidding. The waters on that side somehow represented danger and I would not go there.

I was surprised at the result of my trial run. I had made

significant headway, but I remained apprehensive over the distance between me and the jet-ski and wasted no effort heading back home. I arrived back just a few notches below panic but I knew it was truly time to end this love/hate relationship. It was time to let it go, yet, I wondered if there was something on the jet-ski that I could use. "I wonder if I can use the seat? I know the guy had it up when he was working on the engine. Suppose I could get it off completely? I would bet that it floats." Sure enough, the seat was hinged at the rear. A spring loaded rod acted as a removable pin between the seat and the frame. I pulled the rod out and the seat was free. "Well, this changes things. If I can position this seat under my abdomen, I will have additional flotation and my arms will be free to stroke." I gripped the seat with one hand on each side and hoisted myself up so that my torso was parallel to the water and two seconds later I was, figuratively, eating dirt. The seat was too small, not designed to be a life raft and not surprisingly, unstable. However, all was not lost. I recalled swimming lessons at the Oak Park Pool. I saw myself as a child, hanging onto a foam board while paddling my feet, and actually moving forward. So, the brain trust assembled here in the middle of the ocean decided to ditch the jet-ski and hang onto the seat. I kicked my feet and legs aggressively and did make headway. Swimming solo was faster, but utilizing the seat was less exhausting than unassisted free style swimming and besides, I didn't want to be left alone.

I swam away from the jet-ski. The most agonizing decision of my life. I said goodbye. As the chasm between us grew wider, I spoke out. "Kiss my ass you lousy prick" and I flipped it the bird. It

felt good to do that, at least momentarily; for what followed, emotionally, I never want to experience ever again in my lifetime.

I kept glimpsing over my shoulder as we went our separate
ways, keeping the jet ski in sight as long as possible. The prospect
of changing my mind and returning to my little ship was still an
option as long as I could see it. To my utter dismay, it changed. It
became a ghost ship. Evil. Lifeless. A harbinger of death. The
death ship. A floating coffin. It was the image of a western ghost-
town depicted in the movies. Tumbleweed blowing down the
middle of town. Clapboards banging against the frames of de-
serted structures. Eerie. Desolate. Empty windows to a life that
once was— and now, no longer a hint of humanity. It was, without
precedence the loneliest moment of my life.

The umbilical cord was gone. There was no longer a con-
nection and it was laughing at me. It wasn't home anymore. It was
the enemy and soon it disappeared forever.

The incredible anxiety that the disappearance of the jet ski
created was compounded by my body's progressive deterioration
from exhaustion and exacerbated by the total lack of water. My
esophagus and chest were dry and burning. I could not lubricate
my throat. I saw inside my body and it was like a desert floor,
parched and split open from lack of water. I knew little of the
process of dehydration and what to expect symptomatically. How
long does it take to die from the depletion of body fluids? I so
wanted to intellectualize the succession of events, to put names
on each new bodily disorder, and regretted that I knew so little of
the human body. I wanted to know how long I would live so as to

adjust my survival plan accordingly. This was another item on my wish list, and with historical perspective, of absolutely no value, for I had no control, no plan, no hope. I knew it would take a miracle to alter the outcome of this circumstance. But, I still believed I could affect the outcome.

My chest hurt so bad. Goddammit, my chest hurt so bad.

The seat and I embarked on a new journey west. With us came a wide variety of friends, small friends, fortunately. Little fish nibbling tentatively at my body. More like kisses really. From a few inches to over a foot in length, they became my constant companions. They hung around in the water beneath the seat and I would pet them. I was in awe of their balance and poise as they maintained steady proximity to my body, —and I talked to them.

"Hey fellas. How ya doin'? You're my friends now. Keep the big guys away from me." They were with me for a day, and I was grateful for their companionship.

Never, never, never, did I put my face down into the water and look down. I did not want to see what was in the water or see how deep it was. I would have been struck with the enormity of the ocean and feared that I would become crippled with terror. I did not trust my mind. I no longer had a foundation of logic, reason, or dominion. Rational thought was long gone. Panic was always on the horizon. I believed it was the precursor to death. I didn't want to go there. I preferred to die on my own terms.

"Chuck Muer. The famous restaurateur. Missing with his wife and friends in the Atlantic." It was written in the paper that his daughter had launched an exhaustive search for her father and mother and had turned up nothing. They were rich! She had unlimited resources, yet they all vanished without a trace.

"Liz will get airplanes, but she can't possibly marshal the forces that were at the disposal of the Muer family. What a nice man he was. There's no way I'm going to survive this. If Chuck Muer couldn't make it, how the hell can I?"

I felt bad about Chuck Muer and couldn't shake the feeling of regret over his death. Liz was an employee of the C.A. Muer Corporation at one time and we had occasion to have breakfast at the St.Clair Inn with Mr. Muer and a handful of fellow employees. We were all the richer for the experience. I had been in awe of his success and his gentle demeanor but now we shared a common fate. As I kicked toward the horizon I remarked to myself that "he had simply preceded me."

"I think it's time to get rid of this ring. It's really bothering me. It has no value here or on earth. Even if I make it back, so what, it's useless," empty words from a feeble mind as I removed the ring from my finger, turned it over in my hand and contemplated throwing it away. "This is a test, isn't it? This is not a ring, this is a representation of my life. This is a worldly possession without which— a sign of impending death. If I get rid of it I will be more naked, a return to the beginning of life. I'm not ready yet and I'm not giving in. Killing me will not come free. Besides, I can't see losing a perfectly good ring to the bottom of the ocean. What a waste. If they find my body, at least my wife can sell the ring." Talk about being screwy in the head. At least I still had my basic priorities in order.

Then there was the matter of God. My spiritual life had always been filled with inconsistency and ambiguity, a mixture of faith, habit, indoctrination and contradiction. Until now there had been no need to synthesize a coherent blend of all the bits and pieces.

"What do I do about God? Are you there? I don't see you and I don't feel you." It was not my habit to pray despite the fact that I went to church almost every day of my school life. Stefanie and Joey attended Guardian Angels School and the parish was an integral part of our lives. My best friend and his wife were then and remain now, quite vocal in their commitment to Jesus Christ. Although we attended church every Sunday I did not spend much time contemplating the role of God in my life. I always questioned the role of Roman Catholic Doctrine and its adversarial relationship to the theory of Evolution, which seemed much less a theory than scientific fact. How does one reconcile the birth of Adam and Eve and their descendants as the creation of God and the beginning of human existence when evidence of the evolutionary process was so compelling and impossible to ignore. A matter of faith? Those individuals of unquestioned faith and deep religious conviction would suggest that this is so. It was not my desire to engage in a debate with myself over the issue of God's existence and his role in my life, except that I was in immediate danger of dying and needed help.

"Pray? How can I pray? I have never asked for help from God. Ever the pragmatist, I thought "how can I ask for help from a God whose very existence I doubt, especially under these condi-

tions. Beg for help? No way. I don't beg and I don't snivel." My
reluctance to pray, however, was predicated on the notion of guilt.
Even if it was available, I felt undeserving of God's assistance and
did not feel worthy to receive any special heavenly dispensation. I
could not at this point, however, ignore prayer as a possible option. It felt sacrilegious but I needed all the help I could get.

I settled on a compromise. I would say one Hail Mary and
one Our Father each day. I would not say more than that. The only
problem was that I could not remember the Hail Mary in its en-
tirety and I really wanted to direct my prayers to Mary. So I did my
best each day and I shook my head in disbelief that in spite of the
million times I had said that prayer— I just couldn't get it all. Try
being a Catholic kid and going to confession and one can imagine
the number of times the Hail Mary comes up. "Maybe I'm just stupid and have a low IQ." Oh well, none of that matters now.

In that moment, floating helplessly in the middle of the
ocean, I made a direct pleading to God. "God, if you are going to
kill me, that's okay, but I would like to know either way. I have a
family that doesn't know where I am. They are sick to death and I
cannot live with that. I have a responsibility to them to do my best
to survive. I don't want a slow death. If necessary, lets get it over
with. Otherwise, I'm going to do everything I can to make it home
alive. I won't just sit here and expect you to save me. I will do ALL
that I have to do to save my life. I will have done my very best so
no matter what the outcome if it is in your power to let me live, I
will let your power flow through me."

Aside from my once daily prayers, I planned no further pleas for assistance. At that moment, I must admit I was drawn to the Hail Mary and asked Mary to intervene on my behalf. I never did get that prayer right.

A   N I G H T   T O   R E M E M B E R

Two full days had passed and yet I still had hope and the expectation that someone or something would emerge from the featureless seascape that surrounded me and take me to my family. There had been no external stimuli for much too long. I began to dread the night that soon would fall upon me. The night from hell, to my utter dismay, was coming. I had failed to consider that the weather might change for the worse. It just never dawned on me that the situation could become more dangerous.

"Oh my God, I have to make it through another night but I don't know if I can make it another night." I had to make it just to give the airplanes one last chance to find me. "It will be over tomorrow, but I had to make it through the night to see what the day would bring. My body had deteriorated to the point that I figured I had one more day at best. It was no longer a question of positive thinking. No, this was a realistic assessment of my body wasting away and an educated guess as to how much longer I could endure exposure to the elements without shelter or water.

"Tomorrow is the end, but I will get through the night."

...and what a night it was. If there was a hell on earth, that night was it. If there was a price to pay for salvation, I paid my dues that night. If I am a different person today, as I have been told by those around me, it is as a direct and proximate result of the events of that evening. The line between reality and hallucination disappeared. I could no longer separate, in the words of the Moody Blues, "that which was real and that which was an illusion."

"Time to bunk down for the night. See if you can get some sleep tonight." I pulled the bathing suit liner over my face, pinched the seat between the inside of my arms, clasped the bottom edge of the seat with each hand and closed my eyes. That didn't last long. Sleep? Was I even awake? Was I conscious? There was no frame of reference to establish the difference between the conscious and subconscious state. The sustained repetition of the sea's movement over an extended period of time had produced an altered state of consciousness. Perhaps all of this was an illusion. Was I already dead and didn't know it? The origin of thoughts that flooded my mind remain elusive. Were these thoughts of a conscious mind, hallucinations, or merely dreams and nightmares? I had no way of knowing. Alas, it was unimportant to put a handle on it.

Night had returned. I gazed at the sparkling night sky and set the compass markings in my mind. Heading due West, with the moon at my back, the chilly night breeze was the only unwelcome element in an otherwise beautiful night.

Sometime in the middle of the night the weather did change for the worse. The seas became angry. In the midst of turbulent waters it became difficult to breathe without swallowing mouthfuls of dry salty water. The only thing saving me was the bathing suit, the liner acting as a barrier from the water, allowing me to breathe without gulping large quantities of water. I was thrown about with increased violence, the waves crashing louder and louder, punching me in the head again and again and driving me crazy.

It began to rain. "Rain? Wait a minute, rainwater is fresh. Open your mouth and catch some before it stops." It seemed that I was always playing catch up, my mind in slow motion, excruciatingly sluggish in reacting to the actions going on around me. A vicious cycle of diminished capacity followed by a self imposed mental whipping for dereliction of duty and then a frenzied effort to make up for lost ground. I opened my mouth as wide as I could, stiffened my spine and thrust my jaw to the skies. If I was a bird, my mother would surely have dropped a worm into my mouth, such was my posture. I felt only an occasional light drop of rain onto my face. A single drop of water was welcome. I willed the skies to open up with torrential rains but the volume of rainfall increased only minimally. I kept my mouth open while I was being thrashed about. At one point I felt I could taste fresh water only to be slammed with a wave that went right into my mouth, a personal affront to my dignity and proof that a larger power was directing the action. No one could have this much bad luck. I screamed furiously. "Why? God, why are you doing this to me? I am working as hard as I can. Why are you purposely fighting me? Why are you trying to kill me? I just want a little water. No sooner did I taste a little water then you took it away from me." At the top of my lungs, and with unappeasable aggression, I screamed "why are you doing this?" I consumed too much energy in the process of venting my anger and settled down. I had an idea! "Take off the bathing suit and catch water with it!" I removed the bathing suit from my head, wrung it out and held it aloft. I reasoned that I could squeeze it hard enough to force out the salt water and allow the fresh rain water to absorb into the material. I held it up as high as I could and hoped that I could suck the fresh water out of the fabric. "I'm a genius" I remarked. "No survival training and look what you came up with, Dale. Not bad."

That bathing suit weighed 3,000 lbs. if it were an ounce. The seas continued to pound me and soak the bathing suit every few seconds. The waves would just not leave me alone. I did put the material in my mouth and attempt to suck out the little fresh water that may have graced its surface. It was bitter and salty and not the least bit redeeming. There was no fresh water. Another good idea gone to waste. "I am just going to die. I don't even care."

With the bathing suit back on my head, the liner covering my face, my hands on the seat, I proceeded further into the night.

Something about the waters around me was unusual. There was something in the water near me projecting a noise that I had not heard before. Instead of the normal rolling motion of the seas, I perceived an expediency of movement, difficult to verbalize but best described as a certain volume and percussion. Bump. Felt but not seen. I remember saying to myself, "that is a very large living thing." My intuition told me they were whales as I didn't detect malicious intent. I was merely an oddity and the subject of casual interest on the part of some very large species of marine life. I didn't even know if there were whales in the Gulf of Mexico. That day, I preferred to believe they were whales.

The Condo was beautiful. Two story, painted stark white, balcony on the second floor. Nice new appliances, large rooms, and on the beach. "Why is there water in the bottom half of the refrigerator? I wondered. "On second glance, the entire Condo is flooded with three feet of water. This is really odd. Why would they be selling a Condominium with water? Oh, I get it. This condo is not on the ground. For one thousand dollars down they will ground it." It made perfect sense to me. How could they sell a condo with all that water?

I grasped the thick twine rope that snaked its way through the condo and pulled myself forward, hand after hand, desperately fighting to remain inside the condo. I slipped away from the front door, past the beach and out into the water as I continued to struggle against the tide. "Time to let the seat go. I don't need it anymore. I've got the condo." I let the seat go and in the next moment of panic grabbed it again, admonished myself for being a crazy fool and hung on for dear life. "Lets make sure we have that condo first."

"Hey Charlie! Charlie! Give me a hand." It was Charlie who was helping me purchase the condo and to whom I was to give the 1,000 dollars. Charlie was my advocate and liaison between me and the sellers. Charlie would remove the water from the condo. Only there was no Charlie and there was no condo and as best I could recall, I knew of no Charlie.

In the instant I called his name, I experienced a physical

separation. I looked at myself from above the surface of the water. I became an observer to a one way conversation and recognized the person doing the speaking as me. I wondered why I was talking to someone by the name of Charlie. I was embarrassed by the public display of confusion and swore to keep quiet.

It was logical to conclude that the ferocious roar of the water was due to the action of waves crashing into land. It seemed unlikely that water against water, wave against wave, could produce such deafeningly loud sound. I was convinced to a degree of certainty, regardless of the condo having slipped from my grasp, that land was very close. I extended my right foot as a ballet dancer would extend a toe to the floor, stretched the tendons in my leg and searched for the ocean bottom. "It must be within reach. I know I can touch bottom. I really don't need the seat anymore. I'll get back to the condo and everything will be okay."

In that delusional moment I did let the seat go. It was gone forever. I emerged from my reverie much later, with the realization that I had committed an irreversible act.

"Oh my God, you lost the seat. You messed up pal," and subsequently, "well, you couldn't swim too good with that stupid thing either. What the hell, maybe you're better off without it."

Later that night, at two o'clock on the locational dial, I spotted colorful lights. It looked like a carnival, very festive and a long, long distance away. I had no energy to swim toward it. More significantly, I had no desire.

T H E   L A S T   D A Y   O N   E A R T H ?

Light peaked out from the line of the horizon, the signal of a new day. No early morning mist, no fog, no dew on the car window. None of the telltale signs of a new day in my world, just the arrival of faint light, a precursor to the arrival of the full, hot sun. Daytime in the cycle of the universe with no thought to my comings or goings. I knew that this would be my last day on earth if I was not saved before the next nightfall and as the universe goes, it just wasn't a very big deal.

I removed the wrist band from my left wrist and with great pomp and circumstance flung it as far as I could manage. "Kiss my ass. I really don't care if anyone identifies my body." Boy, did that feel good.

I knew that it was Sunday. I had been counting the days. I also knew that it was day four. As the later news reports would indicate, and confirmed by my wife, it was actually day three. Somewhere along the line I lost a day. I was convinced that I had begun my Olympic swim on the previous Thursday. My internal clock, the clock with which I gauged my waning physical resources, ran on the four day calendar. It has been very difficult for me to accept what is readily apparent to all parties in this case; that Sunday was day three.

Sunday began like none of the other days. I felt energized. As if I had uttered these words only a moment ago, I said to myself that morning, with conviction, "Dale, today you are going to work as hard as you can. You are going to swim as hard and as long and as consistently as you can and hope for the best."

"Today, you are going to save yourself." —and I began with a strength that was not possible for a man who had been out to sea that long. My arms sliced through the water with powerful, sustained strokes.

As a practical matter, the resumption of my post night swimming and the sudden renewed energy was not without history. It had long been my habit to exercise on a regular basis. I started to exercise as an antidote to the stress created by running a business. It had become a daily regimen. In the preceding 10 years, I attended aerobic exercise classes for a minimum of 4 days per week. I was in top physical condition. No body fat. All lean. I had become addicted to the release of endorphins. Better than drugs. Better than alcohol. I also didn't want to see a fat boy when I looked in the mirror. The reserve of energy that yielded this effort was an affirmation of my dedication to physical fitness. I have since wondered if a larger, heavier, taller, stronger and perhaps less fit man could have survived. Being a small guy in good shape finally paid off.

On the morning of what would be my last day at sea, a woman appeared over my right shoulder and said to me, "Dale, you are to swim in that direction", pointing over my left shoulder.

"Keep going that way. The hotels are in that direction." That woman was Mary Dixon, the manager of Maple Athletic Club, the club to which I had belonged for the prior 5 years. Mary and I had a relationship consisting of a regular exchange of pleasantries and a mutual respect for each other. I was very supportive of Mary's work as the manager of a family owned business. She was a young woman entrusted with much responsibility in her role at the health club, at what I considered to be a young age. She was very efficient and loved by all. Mary also filled in as an aerobic instructor on occasion. I was accustomed to following her directives.

For the next few hours, Mary never left me. Her face appeared constantly, always reminding me to swim in "that direction." I suddenly found myself awakened by the sensation of choking on the salt water I was involuntarily swallowing. As fatigue sapped my strength and consciousness left me I repeated this over and over. My tongue was now stiff. My throat was telling me that everything inside my body was drying up. My chest was burning and sore and I knew the source of any future problem was right there in my chest. It felt darkly odd. The future appeared to have arrived.

Time after time I emerged from a stupor only to discover that I was swimming aimlessly, my arms working free-lance, completely disconnected from my brain, the flow of any meaningful information shut off. My body was operating on auto-pilot with the assistance of Mary who was there reminding me of the right direction. I was turned around constantly, but I always got back on track.

Suddenly, in the direction to which I had been advised to go by Mary—there stood hotels. They weren't all hotels. There were clouds on the horizon along with the hotels. That I was sure of. I knew the difference between clouds and clouds that would have one believe were not clouds. I spent a lot of time as a child, laying in bed at night, gazing at the monsters in the sky. I knew which ones were real and which ones were merely an illusion. I was an expert, having spent countless hours accepting and rejecting as many visions as the imagination of a 10 year old would allow. It was a fertile field. I definitely knew my clouds.

My mind began to entertain itself with the most unlikely and bizarre substitutes for reality. I found myself cast as the leader of a regiment of soldiers swimming into battle. I swam around my troops with bluster, willing the soldiers into their synchronous movements by the sheer force of my personality. Before long, I began to question the wisdom of appointing me a leader of men soon to enter the heat of battle.

Wait. I can't do this. I'm dying. These are not soldiers. I'm not an officer. I became aware, not of soldiers, but rather, white caps, each in perfect order fanning out in all directions. Then, I was offered a small boat and a buoy to climb onto. I really tried to climb onto that buoy as it swayed to and fro, the beacon at the top swinging close to the surface as the base was swallowed in the opposite direction; only to repeat its back and forth motion in time with the motion of the seas. Like everything else, an illusion. Reality had become nothing more than a series of mirages, hallucinations, and deceptions. There was nothing left for me to believe in.

M A D N E S S   A N D   M I R A C L E S

Chafed at the armpits and upper back below the arms by the lifejacket, and driven completely crazy spittin' mad by the constant irritation, I gave up on my military career and continued swimming in earnest, in the wrong direction of course.

Then came another apparition as if from nowhere. A ship appeared. The most beautiful ship I have ever seen. It tempted me with its beauty and offered refuge from a watery grave. I swam toward the ship and yelled for help. I could not discern specific features but knew it to be a passenger vessel, a cruise ship. It was very white, its outline a blur, its central brilliance diminished in concentric circles radiating outward toward its outer edge. It was only half a mile away in my best estimation as I removed the bathing suit from my head and began waving for help. Swimming and screaming and hollering and waving and in the blink of an eye, it disappeared. There was nothing on the horizon. I was dumbstruck with the realization that it had disappeared before my very eyes. I was certain that I was close enough to have been heard.

I began to cry.

It took me two years to admit to myself that that ship never existed. I had never doubted or even questioned its existence until that moment. Only a fool could ignore the spiritual and mystical significance of that ship. Only a fool could ignore its real intent, for the vision of that ship was nothing more than an invitation to eternity. I was, however, not allowed to board that vessel. My fate remained a life on earth.

None of these alleged intellectual or emotional hypotheses had any impact at the time. I was just plain miserable as I turned away from the spot where the ship had once stood and resumed my journey west.

Nothing in my life prepared me for what was next. As I began to turn toward the west I felt something slither up my left leg at the ankle. "Oh my God, SNAKES."

"I hate snakes. I am scared to death of snakes. I only felt one but I assumed there were others, the area around me was instantly beset with sea life as thick as vegetable soup. Misery generally keeps a lot of company. "I can't believe this is happening. First the ship disappears and then snakes. What am I going to do?" The snake slithered around my leg like the stripes on a barber pole as it rose toward my knee.

After all that I had faced, this was the most unspeakable horror. This intruder was insinuating itself into my reality, silent, unseen, but palpable and sinister. Then I began to see the prospect of a lethal bite delivered by this serpent as a respite from the uncertainty I had been facing.

"Maybe this is the time for me to die. If this snake is venomous and bites me, then I'll die and this will be all over. This could be okay."

I quickly discarded that fatalistic analysis and began a brief dialogue. "I am not going to look at you, but you are going to get off my leg." With those words, I reached down below the surface of the water and grabbed the snake with my left hand determined to lift it above the surface of the water and fling it as far as possible. I raised my arm and hand above the surface, vowing not to look, as I turned my face away and in one desperate motion I threw the snake away. It could not have landed far from me, and could easily find its way back to me, but it was all that I could do.

Whether from its own fear or lack of interest, the snake never returned and I was relieved to be alone again but I was very angry and unwilling to accept that this was happening to me. "What had I done in life to deserve this? Why is this happening to me? The physical trauma was a burden. The psychological stresses were much graver. In less than 15 minutes I had been abandoned by a rescue ship and visited by the grim reaper in the guise of a serpent.

Then I was visited again as there appeared a single bird in the afternoon sky. A singular black bird. That black bird, but for the ever-present sea creatures, was the only sign of life. At that moment it could only have represented death. A vulture. Circling. Waiting. There had not been a sign of life for three days. No flies, no bugs, no flocks of geese in the sky flying in perfect formation to some unknown destination. ...and then a lone black vulture. Waiting for me to die. I yelled at the bird. "Get the F out of here. You are not going to get me. Not yet, anyway."

Mercifully, just like the snake, that bird left shortly thereafter, never to return.

I could barely lift my arms as I continued swimming west, another blistering day, the sun out in full force.

I still embraced the notion that a sign of life would somehow appear in the distance. However innocent or naive it was, I believed that salvation would show up on the horizon, even in my darkest moments and those were indeed, dark moments. The last time I had seen a human being was over three days past. But in spite of dehydration, incredible longing for drink, hallucinations, snakes, exhaustion, loneliness and despair, I was still alive.

Barely.

It was at that moment in my journey that I experienced what I refer to as a window to the universe. I shall attempt to describe that which I have found difficult to translate to words, an event which I have not felt since, a segue' to the final moment of life on earth, a bridge to the next experience, an experience so profoundly transcendental that I cannot describe it but merely talk about it in some general philosophical sense.

I was at once seeing the true nature of my existence with unprecedented clarity. It became clear that human beings do not occupy a prominent position in the universe. Our ability to process information, rationalize various thoughts, and enjoy a full range of emotions is all well and good for the duration of our life on earth. In the universe at large, however, and at the moment of our death, we become part of the energy of the universe. Our minds become an energy source as we experience a transition from our human bodies into our role as another seed of energy in the universe of limitless electrical energy. No emotion, no rationale, none of the thought processes that occupy our every waking moment as living, breathing people. Simply power. Vibrations of energy coursing through and around us as we become a part of the landscape of energy that fills the space around us.

These thoughts were merely an adjunct to a real physical episode at sea on that final day prior to my rescue. In what I refer to as "the moment of my death," I experienced the phenomenon of my mind and body pulling away from the surface of the ocean, my eyes viewing the earth as smaller and smaller as I looked upon the world much like an astronaut looking at the earth through the porthole of a spacecraft. It became clear that my life was so insignificant. The plans, dreams, and machinations of everyday life were about nothing. The transition from the human experience to a new role as part of an immense energy field, was before me, and it was okay. No worried anticipation, no fear, no concern over leaving the human condition. It was just plain beautiful. It seemed the most natural thing in the world. At what seemed a million miles per hour, with my back to the sky and my eyes wide open to the earth and the water before me,— the Gulf of Mexico, the North American Continent, the earth itself became progressively smaller and smaller as I pulled away; my life force pouring into a fabric of energy, a quilt of infinite power suspended in space and capable of absorbing my life, and sustaining its power.

Right before my very eyes.

Gradually, I left this magical state and returned to the wretched reality of my struggle to be found at sea. But all I wanted to do was go back to where I had been. A few years have now passed and I am secure in my belief that what I experienced cannot be dismissed as the hallucinations of an exhausted, delirious, dehydrated, lunatic castaway. As of this writing, I remain ready and willing to return and stand firmly convinced of the reality of my vision.

It is this singular event that has changed my views of God from the conventional notion of a supreme being watching over his minions, flanked by Jesus Christ who died for our sins. I saw no signs of God. I saw nothing that would indicate the existence of a soul rising to heaven. And I remain, paradoxically, anxious that I have taken a position that is an opposite extreme to the beliefs of my close friends and family. It is, nonetheless, a true accounting of the aftermath of my experience at sea. I can only offer my deepest apologies to those who know me best, that I have chosen to embrace a view of eternity that defies convention.

W H O   W O U L D   E V E R
B E L I E V E ?

Mid afternoon of a hot sun drenched sky and I was convinced that I had swum into a fresh water stream crossing my path.

"Dale, you know better than to drink the salt water" I remarked to myself. "But, this is fresh water! Look! There's seaweed here." True enough, a few small sprigs of what appeared to be a small plant floated in front of me. I was convinced that a current of fresh water coursed through this area. I grasped the plant in my hand and examined it closely in hopes of extracting any fresh nourishment from its core. It appeared to have some immature berry pods from which I could suck its inner sweetness. I raised the pod to my mouth and sucked to its core only to discover that it was bitter and lacking any life sustaining qualities. Just the garden variety seaweed after all.

I felt confident that the water before me was now fresh. "Don't fall for that shit. You know that it's salt water. You're becoming mentally weak. Don't drink it. You're going to die if you do; but it really is sweet. It's not salt water." Back and forth in a seesaw of emotions, struggling with a solution to the question before me. The last vestige of common sense, some innate sensibility remained in a mind ravaged from three days of exposure and I did not drink the water. How I did not succumb to the overwhelming temptation to drink the ocean water is another mystery for which I have no answer. It was a significant, tangible moment and on the short list of Kodak moments.

I sought sustenance by returning to thoughts of love for my wife and children. I was still convinced they were looking for me. I scanned the skies for airplanes, dreamed for a drink, and went back to work, determined to prove to everyone that I could survive. "I'm gonna come out of this water and everyone is going to know I am the toughest guy they ever met. I'm going to prove it."

C O K E   O R   P E P S I   O R   P E E ?

It occurred to me that the appearance of seaweed in the waters before me was an un-natural phenomenon. "How is it that I have been out here for three or four days and this is the first time I have seen seaweed? Could my perception of having crossed a fresh water stream have a much simpler answer? Perhaps this is the trail of a cruise ship, and the seaweed is floating on the surface after having been cut loose from the prop of a ship."

I began to convince myself that a cruise ship had passed through the area. I also knew that cruise lines had a practice of dumping garbage overboard. "Maybe I will come across something of value." What appeared to be a bleach bottle floated up. I grasped its handle, looked inside, determined it was of no value and tossed it aside.

My very next thought was, "wouldn't it be a miracle if a bottle floated up and the lid was on it? And wouldn't it really be a miracle if it had something to drink in it?" And then suddenly as if my thoughts had conjured up a pop bottle, there it was. Like Kreskin bending the spoon with his mind, a Coke bottle, lid intact—— floated within my reach.

I snatched it from the water, held it aloft, and discovered a half inch of clear fluid of indeterminate origin inside. What a break. I looked at the liquid with the rays of the sun shining through the bottle illuminating its contents. I couldn't wait to taste it. The cap was encrusted with what I assumed to be mollusks and other sea life that normally attaches itself to the bottom of ships. I broke the cap free and licked its inner surface to pick up any moisture that may have splashed onto its surface. I then looked at the meager amount of liquid in the bottom of the bottle and grinned from ear to ear. "Not much in here, but this is going to save me. I am going to drink this in two sips. The first phase will be a carefully measured sip where I will coat as much of my esophagus and inner lining as I can. The second sip will be for pure pleasure." I put my nose to the bottle and smelled. I couldn't tell what it was. It smelled like urine, but it had a faint odor of perfume. I decided that urine or not, I was going to drink this stuff. "I don't care if some guy pissed in this bottle because he couldn't find a bathroom and then threw it overboard," which was the prevailing thought of the moment. There was so little that it did not seem logical someone would urinate in the bottle. If a guy had to go that bad, it would be more than half full. Besides, it had that perfumy smell. It was most likely a matter of the sun having baked the plastic bottle and bleached the Coke as it floated along the surface of the ocean. I couldn't have cared less. I was going to drink that stuff.

That first sip was like nothing I had ever tasted. I lingered over the second tiny sip after allowing the first to irrigate my throat.

Compared to the amount of liquid in that bottle, a full shot glass would have looked generous in comparison, but it did the job. With fat, blistered lips and a sandpaper tongue, I thrust my tongue into the top of the bottle and tried to lick whatever I could from the inner surface of the bottle. There was really nothing there, but failure to extract even one droplet of liquid would be negligent. My tongue had no feeling. I held it with my fingers. It could have belonged to someone else.

With a mind made lucid by each droplet, I screwed the cap back onto the bottle and threw it away, ever so grateful for that precious little bottle of life. I knew it wasn't enough to soothe the savage beast that burned red hot within my body but it was a beginning and a positive affirmation that I was going in the right direction, literally.

I returned to the business at hand, my illusionary survival mode. I tried to orient myself. "You are facing west. Land is at 10:00 on the locational dial. Keep swimming in that direction." That I did, hour after hour, all the while gazing at the clouds on the horizon, confident that there were Hotels interspersed within those clouds, and then with the next thought—not believing any of it for a minute. "There is nothing on that horizon except for clouds. You are dying. There is zero chance of there being hotels out there."

That bleak perception of reality was not consistent with my survival and I knew it. If I simply gave up and stopped swimming I would die miserably. On the other hand, if I kept working, kept digging, kept looking ahead and swimming forward, at least there was a chance. There was always a chance. I would at least die with my eyes blazing. I would not give up.

Except for the darkest moments, I always embraced the belief that a sign of life would appear in the distance. A subconscious belief, or more appropriately what I would define as an 'intuitive expectancy'. In retrospect, this was an expectancy born of merciful innocence, or perhaps blissfull ignorance, but necessary for me to prevail.

With those thoughts predominant, another chapter in my experience at sea began to unfold. Not immediately, for the order of the day was to resume swimming, but in the very near future. Good things were about to happen.

W H O   A R E   Y O U ?

I had been swimming since daybreak with Mary Dixon's guidance and encouragement and it had finally paid off. Late Sunday afternoon and there they were. There were hotels off in the distance exactly where I knew they'd be.

I saw them as I rose to the crest of another wave. Anxious to verify my sighting, I paddled furiously as I rode down into the bottom of the wave and back up again to its peak.

There they were—and not just the hotels. I saw a beautiful woman in a black one piece bathing suit with her husband riding a small wind surfer, having fun in front of the resort. "Those are hotels after all!"

I knew I had to get their attention quickly. I needed to let them know that I was there. This had to be an all out effort.

With that in mind, I removed the bathing suit from my head and began yelling and swinging the suit back and forth. The back end of a truck would have been lighter. My arms couldn't do it. I just didn't have the strength, but did have enough presence of mind to figure out that the bathing suit would be much lighter if it weren't soaked. So, I wrung it out in much the same fashion as

I had done a few days earlier when attempting to catch rain water, and as I rode to the crest of each successive wave, I continued to wave as much as I could. It was nearly impossible to keep the suit from getting soaked and my fortunes rose and fell with the top and bottom of each swell. I finally gave up waving and resumed swimming in their direction.

"That isn't a woman windsurfing. It's too big. It's a small pleasure craft, or a charter fishing boat."

It wasn't a pleasure craft or a fishing boat.

Looming large and headed straight for me was a ship the size of which I had never seen. There was actually a chance I could be rescued. As the ship steamed toward me I raised my left arm and jerked it up and down in a movement like a child standing on a freeway overpass imploring the truck drivers to blast their horn. Indeed, I was a child, helpless and hoping beyond hope that they would see me and hit that horn.

"Come on, let me know that you see me." I mouthed those words over and over as I continued to alternately wave my purple bathing suit and pantomime the blast of a horn. As the ship advanced closer and closer, and without my presence having been acknowledged, I decided to take action. They were nearly on top of me when I came to the conclusion that I would attempt to grab onto the ship when it reached me.

"If I can grab onto the V of the ship, with the V centered directly in the middle of my body and with my arms stretched on both sides of the ship, I should be able to hold on and slowly worm my way up to the deck. The forward motion of the ship will

keep me from falling off as I slither up. I have to hit it just right
though. If I'm too far one way or the other it'll throw me off."

The ship was nearly on top of me and bearing down faster
than I was prepared to handle. I did not have the luxury of engag-
ing in an internal debate over the wisdom of a plan to scurry up
the prow. Some sixth sense told me that my plan was the stupidest
thing I could ever think of. "Forward motion? What an idiot." It
became readily apparent that I had better get out of the way. NOW.

Wham! I hadn't even made the final decision to swim out
of the way when I was slammed by the water coming off the side
of the ship as it pounded forward. The wall of water slapping my
back was violent, but it was new and I welcomed it. I swam as fast
as I could for fear of being sucked back into the hole in the water
created by the ship. It was probable that I would be sucked down
into the hole, get repeatedly bounced on and off the hull of the
ship as it passed forward, get sucked down into the screws, chewed
up and sprayed out the back of the blades. Shark chum for sure.

Once again, I managed to escape from harms way; and found
myself staring at a wall of steel. I had never seen a wall of steel,
higher than a tall building, moving past me no more than ten
feet away.

Looking almost straight up I could only see more steel. There
may have been a deck up there somewhere, but I wouldn't have
bet on it.

"They still can't see me. How the hell can they not see me?"
I didn't have my glasses on, but "surely someone should be able
to see me." I knew there was a tower of glass at the rear of the

ship, having earlier spotted it from a distance. In fact, it was the tower of glass, which I presumed to be the nerve center of the ship, that I had previously directed my waving and horn honking. The rear of the ship was approaching quickly. I was later told that this ship, the MS Almania was travelling at 15 knots. From my position, in the water, and only a few feet away, this was a blazing speed. There was no indication of having been seen, and I mouthed the words "this ship will pass me in a moment."

"Help me. Help! Help! Help! Over and over I yelled as best I could, praising the little bottle of piss that had given my throat some relief and allowed me to project sounds somewhat above a horse whisper. "Is that me yelling?" Did I tell myself to yell?"

I looked up at the glass house that stood at least four or five stories high, the sun's rays bouncing off its surface, and could see absolutely nothing.

It was a two way street, for there was no sign of life within the confines of that ship of glass and steel, and they could not see the likes of one insignificant little bastard whose last hope for life on earth resided a mere 50 feet away.

"I have come all this way and I am not going to make it. I have struggled for four days. Ships don't get bigger than this. If this ship couldn't see me, no one will see me. Only the second sign of mankind in four days and it's over. There won't be any airplanes. They can't see me anyway. It won't even matter if another ship comes by. They will never see me either. It's all over."

The ship passed by without me.

With the emotions of a madman, or perhaps, final reconciliation, I began to laugh. It was all over.

"What a relief. The end of my life is not as I would have written it, but at least I have a final answer. There is no further speculation. I'm done now. It's okay."

I grinned from ear to ear as I watched the ship pass into the distance. I could see its rear end and came to the realization that I never did have a chance. "All that work for nothing. Oh well. At least I tried."

"I really don't want to prolong this any more than necessary." I raised my right arm from the surface of the water, gazed at my wrist and contemplated tearing the vein from beneath the surface of the skin with my teeth. "With sufficient aggression, I should be capable of biting deep enough to extract a major blood vessel and quickly bleed to death. The sharks will surely ravage my dead body, but whether it's now or tomorrow morning won't make much difference. I don't want to go through another night and I'll be dead in the morning anyway."

T H E   G E R M A N S

In the distance, faint but intelligible, I heard the words "Man overboard."

From the top floor of the structure perched upon the rear end of the ship I could see a figure throwing a ring followed by what appeared to be a lantern or buoy of some sort.

"They had seen me after all."

Inexplicably, I felt no sense of joy or relief at my prospects for salvation but rather, numb indifference. I do not know how to explain this complete lack of feeling. I remain indifferent toward most things to the present day and can only speculate that having been to the gates of the abyss, not much else matters. Emotionally, I had moved out. Life on earth was in my past. No longer important. No longer all consuming.

"Why are they throwing a ring out into the water? I don't need a ring. I'm doing just fine. I've stayed afloat this long." Their actions seemed meaningless.

"What's that thing attached to it? Oh, I know! It IS a little buoy and it must have a light so it can be seen at night."

Then I understood. They were really busy. "They're businessmen like me. They don't have time to stop and pick me up. I get it. Why else would they keep going? That is as it should be." They were indeed a long way off. The back end of that ship must have been a half mile away.

"That's alright. I know what it's like to be busy. I've been in business. It must cost a lot of money to stop a ship. Imagine the fuel cost. Like landing an airplane mid-flight to pick up one passenger. I understand."

It then occurred to me that they were stopping. "Maybe stopping a ship is like stopping a train, it takes a while. That must be it. They must be slowing down." In fact, I could see the front of the ship turning slightly to the right.

All I could think to do was mutter "Hmmn" to myself. I couldn't bring myself to action. I remained in place, busy thinking, a whirlwind of thoughts. Thinking of everything and nothing at the same time. Electric currents crisscrossed my mind with thoughts of who knows what. I was talking nonsense and gibberish with brief pictures of me busy talking to myself; interspersed with momentary bits of clarity.

It was during one of those moments of clarity that it struck me that I had an obligation to swim toward the ship. They were, afterall, waiting for me. I began to swim furiously as I felt very bad that they would be inconvenienced by my presence.

In another flash of clarity I remembered what for many days had been irrelevant. I was aware, as I was about to be delivered to safety, that I was naked.

"Wait Dale. You're naked. You can't go on that ship naked.

No way. You could get in trouble if there are women aboard." So, I decided to remove the bathing suit from my head and put it on. My legs were so stiff that what should have been a very simple process seemed nearly impossible.

"Oh no. I can't get this suit on. They are probably looking at me and wondering why I am not making an effort. They must think I am lazy. I'm not lazy. I have to put something on."

With those critical thoughts in mind, I began to cry. I could not take the pressure. I just wanted to be left alone. This was a watershed moment of self deprecation and inadequacy that haunts me to the present.

With tremendous difficulty, I did get the bathing suit on and resumed swimming in the direction of the ship. When I arrived within shouting distance of the side of the ship, someone called out asking if I was capable of climbing up a jacobs ladder. I had no clue what a jacobs ladder was, but I knew I couldn't climb any kind of ladder. I shook my head negatively.

I watched with incredulous curiosity as a large hydraulic boom swung out to pick up a large red, metal boat from the deck of the ship and lower it into the water. The deep, throaty roar of powerful engines filled the air and in a matter of seconds, the posse had arrived...

Four dark skinned men leaned over the side of the craft, threw out a rope ladder and encouraged me to climb aboard. I had no strength and could not do so.

They reached down, grabbed me under the armpits and plucked me from the waters. With excruciating pain from their rough hands, I was thrown onto the floor of the boat, and we headed back to the mother ship.

I lay upon a lengthy coil of dirty, greasy rope, my back, head, arms, and legs pressed into the deck like magnets. The rope dug painfully into my skin and I lay there powerless. I had no strength to move to a more comfortable position and wondered why they had treated me so poorly. With hardly the movement of an eyelash, my expression a lifeless mask, I gazed up at the men running the boat and wondered why they had treated me with such haste and indifference. It seemed they had treated me with disdain and a patent lack of interest in my comfort. In reality, it was a rescue situation on the high seas. No talk. All action. As it were, I was being handled as best they could manage, a big lifeless fish who couldn't help them a bit. I was at their mercy and decided that I didn't have it so bad after all.

I was actually out of the water for the first time in many, many days. This moment is branded on my consciousness forever, the crew of the small rescue vessel tying up to the overhead boom, followed by our ascent to the deck of the mother ship. From high above, he grasped the railing and leaned forward with the demeanor of a man plainly at home in that environment. With a thick, unmistakable German accent, the ship's Captain bellowed, "Who are you?"

I didn't answer. I just didn't feel like it and I didn't know how. "Hey I'm Dale Chimenti, you know-President of American Freezer, business executive, successful guy—all the important stuff." No answer was much better. I was too tired anyway.

The rescue vessel stopped somewhere on the main deck. I vaguely recall being carried to an open air room or covered area on the outside of the ship and being laid out on a table. The Captain entered the area and asked, "How long have you been in the Ocean?"

I replied, "4 days." The room sprang to life with reactions of incredulity. The crew was flabbergasted that I could have been in the water so long. Some of the crew members said that I was swimming so powerfully that it was assumed that I was a crew member who had just fallen from the ship. The captain expressed shock and asked, "Are you the Jet Skier?" With my reply his face registered the look of one who had just solved the puzzle; for he had been notified in a transmission sent out by the U.S. Coastguard to all ships in the Gulf of Mexico, Caribbean, and South Atlantic to be on the lookout for a white male/40 who had gone into the water on a JetSki/17Feb. Captain Volquard Richter, MS Almania had, earlier, categorically dismissed said report. His ship, on a course for the east coast of the United States was at least 125 miles north of the nearest landmass, the Yucatan Peninsula. He did not give the notice a second glance.

There were countless crew members attending to me. They lifted my head up and pressed a glass to my lips. Water. I had hoped, but never realistically expected that I would taste water again, but there it was...damn. I had beaten the odds. Quietly, I began to laugh...

I remain baffled over the events that unfolded that day. The events of that day were nothing short of miraculous. Unexplainable in simple human terms. Unbelievable odds for those beholden to chance. As to a statistical probability? Off the charts. Impossible for those given to cynicism. Perfectly plausible for those steeped in faith. For me, something that simply was. My role,—— the narrator of a true life story, and the beneficiary of an experience that has touched millions of people in, hopefully, a positive way, everyone free to interpret the circumstance of my rescue in their own way.

THE MOTHER SHIP

The crew began to remove my bathing suit when I noticed a woman standing a few strides from the head of the table upon which I lay. "So much for putting on my bathing suit." The Captain, recently married, had brought his wife along for this voyage. A beautiful woman no less and there I was in all my naked glory, and not looking great. The reader can't imagine what it looks like to be pickled in brine and baked under a heat lamp for what turned out to be a total of 3 days, but it wasn't pretty. I had lost 15 lbs., and my face resembled a lunar landscape, with white pus oozing from pimply craters, my lips swollen and cracked, the skin on my arms coming off in sheets. Oh well, it could have been much worse.

Captain Richter took control, allowing me only a small taste of water, concerned that my body would react poorly to the ingestion of too much liquid all at once. He scooped me up and carried me to my own quarters, a warm cocoon located somewhere in the interior of the ship.

He sat me on a chair in the shower and bathed me, rinsing away the salt water from my body.

He gave me his clothes.

He carried me to my bunk and placed me in the bed, and I am forever grateful for this big bear of a man who saw to my every need and did more for my convalescence than I could ever imagine, this complete stranger, who in his goodness, remained steadfast in his attentiveness to my rehabilitation. There were no medical personnel aboard ship, however, the Captain and I agreed that aside from severe dehydration, there was no need for off-site emergency care. We were a long way from civilization. I suspect that he would have alerted the U.S. Coast Guard for assistance upon entering U.S. waters if I were in trouble. He indicated that his ship, the MS Almania was on a course for Port Everglades, Florida—some two days away. No argument from me. I didn't want to move.

I could not get enough liquid. Captain Richter brought can after can of apple juice, grape juice, and water. I drank it all very quickly. These were the large serving cans, not individual vends and I could not get enough. I wanted orange juice. They warned me not to drink orange juice because of the citrus but I wouldn't listen. I got my orange juice. I also hurt real bad. Big hurt. The orange juice hit my lips like hydrochloric acid. It burned like no other burn. I should have listened. The empty cans cluttered the table in my quarters like bowling pins scattered to and fro.

Mid evening of the first day aboard ship the Captain arrived at my quarters to inform me that we were within range of a phone call. It seemed odd that given the state of the prevailing technology we could not make a call until we were "in range," but he indicated that I could now call the mainland and inquired if I were capable of coming up to the pilot house. I nodded affirmatively and asked him to show the way. He warned me that it was 4 flights of stairs. He preferred that I not try it. I insisted. Against his judgement, I began the ascent to the top floor using the tubular steel railing for support and lifted myself up very slowly on treads one could have eaten off of. I have never seen a place so clean in my life. Spit shine clean without a hint of dust. I made it to the bridge under my own power.

The bridge was a very large room which I estimated to be 30 feet square with glass panels running a few feet from the floor all the way up to the ceiling, affording a spectacular view of a deck the size of a football field as well as the ocean and horizon beyond. The floor was a green tile so shiny it glared. With a subdued and solemn air the ship's officers went about their business. Relaxed, but all business. It was definitely not a pleasure craft.

I was directed past a large drafting type table, with charts spread across its surface, to the communications control area. It was then a question of who to call. I did not remember the name of the Hotel where we were staying and had no idea where my wife might be, so I decided to call my parents. The Captain dialed and handed me the receiver. I had regained in some small measure, my sense of humor. As if I were at the office making my daily casual check-in call, and with my customary cartoon voiced opening dialogue, I said, when my Mother answered, "Hi Ma, what's new?"

My Mother started crying. I felt like a heel. "Ma, how come you're crying? What's going on?"

I didn't get it. "What's the big deal? No problem here." I may have a sense of humor, but at times no common sense. Of course my Mother and Father would be upset. My Mother's crying continued unabated for some time before we finally established that Liz was still at the Hotel in Cozumel. I explained that I was on the S.S Almania headed for Port Everglades, Florida and would arrive within a day or so. She agreed to contact Liz and inform her of my whereabouts. In the meantime, ever the salesman, I jokingly told my Mother to call Bill.

"Hey Ma, why don't you call Bill? Who knows, there may be some local interest. It can't be bad for business."

I chuckled to myself and said my good-byes.

Bill, was Bonds, Bill Bonds; for 20 years the reigning king of network news in the Detroit area. THE anchorman for Channel 7, the ABC affiliate.

Little did I know that the networks, the tabloid news shows, and newspapers from around the country were itching for the story. Boy, did it get interesting in a hurry.

L I Z A B E T H - A R M Y   O F   O N E

The story of Liz's efforts to find me began the moment Danny sped away from me on that first morning of my disappearance. Danny came ashore on his jet-ski after leaving me on that fateful morning and approached Liz, who was on the beach with Stefanie and Joey, merely to provide a running play by play on what he and I were doing. Understandably, Danny was not concerned with my welfare. It was, after all, a warm sunny day and I was just a short distance from shore basking in the sun. He strode toward Liz in a confident manner and appeared to be in an upbeat mood. Liz's take on the situation was anything but carefree. She was immediately aware of the potentially dangerous situation that was developing.

Liz was born and raised in the boroughs of New York City. One hundred percent Irish and with more cousins than should be allowed by law- all of them named Patrick or some variation thereof, they spent their summers at the beach on the Atlantic Ocean. Liz had been a certified lifeguard and she knew full well the unforgiving nature of the open sea. Liz's reaction to Danny's news was instinctively guarded. Her antennae rose as her natural protective reflexes went on full alert status.

In response to Liz's obvious concern Danny quickly returned to the rental shack and informed the staff of the situation. Reluctantly, one of the rental shack employees boarded Danny's jet ski with Danny riding shotgun and in the direction of where Danny had last seen me. They spent 20-30 minutes looking for me and then returned to shore empty-handed. Their method of search and rescue was as effective as pointing to the sky and trying to find the black hole.

At that moment I am sure Danny would have rather faced the devil than to deal with Liz. Liz, who was now officially alarmed, met them at the dock and approached the Mexicans with a mission in mind. They were not in the mood to deal with her and would simply not listen to her requests to take a boat out and conduct a genuine search. Danny remained apparently unconcerned and tried to treat the matter as merely problematic, not life threatening. Had I been in his place, with little or no seafaring knowledge, I too perhaps would have been unmoved by Liz's protestations.

"Your husband go too far," the people at the rental shack exclaimed. They should have known better to even think those thoughts let alone say the words.

Apparently maintaining their entrepreneurial window of opportunity they continued to accept deposits and make arrangements for the scuba divers who now scurried about the dock loading the boat with an assortment of air tanks, masks and other diving equipment, seemingly oblivious to Liz's pleadings to treat this as a true emergency. She figured out in a hurry that a macho and 'manana' attitude prevailed and that they were not going to listen to a woman. She pulled Danny aside and asked him to take the lead in "convincing the bastards to quit taking any more money and get going." Danny finally convinced them to take him out in the boat. It took them 40 minutes to unload the scuba gear and go for chicken and beer to sustain their upcoming rescue efforts. Lunch was very important. Beverages too.

After 90 minutes of searching, Danny and the Mexicans returned to the dock empty handed. "We didn't find him Liz," Danny offered, "but don't worry it's only 2:00. There is plenty of time to find him."

Liz would not be appeased by this reassurance. I believe Liz will remain, until her dying moment, very angry over the treatment she received from the hotel management and the local Mexican officials. She saw their ministrations for what they were, a transparent shell game offered merely to placate another troublesome American tourist, and with malicious intent, to undermine her efforts to save her husband's life. Little did they know, she was just getting started.

Liz asked for the police. "No Policia," they replied. They finally agreed to call the Police after Liz threatened to create an ugly scene. The Police never came. Were they ever called? Conventional wisdom would suggest that the Police were never notified. Liz finally walked to the edge of the road, and flagged down a passing Police car. They spoke Spanish and only enough English to inform Liz that they would not write a missing persons report. "He missing if you say he missing."

She then returned to the rental shack and demanded that something be done. "What about a Coast Guard rescue boat, a helicopter, or an airplane?" She was informed that none of those resources were available.

A Michigan State Policeman, on vacation, offered his help and remained a source of strength for Liz. There was little he could do. His continued presence was enough to at least provide emotional support.

Liz decided that it was time to call the American Embassy, a decision precipitated by a systematic lack of concern on the part of various Mexican officials and Hotel management. She was put in touch with a Mr. John Desmond from the American Consulate. He was, at first blush, unconcerned and pointed out that I was lost in a very busy area with a crush of traffic and would likely be spotted and rescued by a passing boat. "It would be hard for a tourist floating on a disabled jet-ski to go unnoticed in that environment."

He was quick to add that the Mexican Navy had only one boat which was located in Baja California— a world away and that a search by the Mexican government would not be forthcoming.

"Mrs. Chimenti, there is no way your husband could slip through and not be seen. Call me in the morning."

As a footnote, five hours had passed by and Liz knew that night would descend within a few short hours.

Liz returned to the jet-ski rental shack again. There she was introduced to an American citizen by the name of Kelly, whose husband had disappeared a few years earlier in an unexplained scuba incident. Kelly was an employee of the company that operated the rental shack. It was Kelly who acted as interpreter and sometime companion to Liz. It was Kelly to whom Liz turned in seeking an airplane to conduct a search. Since the Mexican government had no help to offer, and in the absence of any government or local rescue plane, Liz asked Kelly to find a private plane for hire— one with searchlights. Kelly informed Liz that there was a plane at the airport in Playa del Carmen that she could hire for $ 300.00 per hour. Searchlights, however, were out of the question. The onset of dusk would put off any further search attempt until the following day.

"Please," Liz implored, "get the airplane now."

With our children Stefanie and Joey placed in the care of a middle-aged couple from Indiana, Liz, Danny, and Kelley took a cab to the airport to meet the pilot who was flying in from Playa del Carmen, another popular resort located on the Mexican mainland southwest of Cozumel.

Liz handed our Visa card to the pilot. Visa's media message notwithstanding, the pilot would not accept the highly vaunted Visa or Mastercard, or if ever offered, a million dollar letter of credit. My seemingly wasteful (75$ x 18 yr.) and purportedly widely accepted American Express Gold card literally became as good as gold. Liz plucked it from my wallet. There were smiles all around.

By mid-afternoon of the first day Liz had an airplane in the air.

It was decided that Danny would go up first. Liz headed back to the Hotel to play with our children on the beach. For the sake of the children she would act the part of a happy doting mother, outwardly carefree and calm. She was later accused by the hotel officials of being unconcerned with the welfare of her missing husband and therefore a co-conspirator with Danny in a plot to murder me. This flimsy fabrication was all for the shameful purpose of justifying their edict forcing Liz out of her room on the last day of her Apple tour.

Now more than ever, Liz needed all of her strength to grapple with the apathetic Mexican mind set in order to mount a serious rescue effort and to continue to care for her two children. Tragically, perhaps triggered by stress, she began to hemorrhage and painfully cramp.

At dusk on the first day Danny and Kelley from the rental shack would return from their aerial reconnaissance with bad news. They had searched for hours and found nothing. "I don't know Liz, I just don't know where he is." Danny was clearly distressed and miserable. He could not believe how ugly the situation had become. He said they had spent the better part of the late afternoon diving up and down, swooping in and out, chasing a variety of debris, each time hoping it was me. The flight had done nothing but burn dollars and daylight while making Danny nauseous, terrified, and desperately frustrated.

Ever the optimist, Liz was sure that with the approaching darkness, I would pop a flare and they would see me. Kelley informed her that there were no flares aboard the jet-ski. In fact, there were no lifesaving devices aboard the jet-ski at all.

With the airplane reserved for 7:00 AM the next morning, Liz left the beach area, walked to the registration desk in the lobby of the hotel and asked for the manager, hoping to enlist him in her search, or anyone who would assist her. She was informed by the desk clerk that the manager was busy and did not have time to see her. News of a guest being lost out in the ocean had been circulating amongst the hotel employees, and the hotel guests, many of whom were American. It would have been impossible for the Hotel management not to have heard. The manager, however, would not grant her an audience. A short time later Liz was informed by the desk clerk that the manager had gone home.

As they were preparing to retire for the night, Stefanie and Joey peered into the darkness from their 7th floor window, waived their hands and said "Night, Night Daddy." Liz had convinced them that "Daddy was just playing hide and seek." Unfortunately, Daddy was easily winning this game.

As light dawned on the second day, Liz was passing large blood clots and was exhausted. She was torn between the need to rescue her husband and the maternal drive to shield her children from the terrible truth of the situation. Liz decided that she would take the first shift up in the airplane while Danny cared for the children and continued the charade.

With a full load of fuel the Cessna was good for about 5 hours in the air. With Antonio at the controls and Kelley seated in the co-pilot seat, Liz sat in the back and pressed the binoculars to her face until her eyes became black and blue. The drone of the engine was interrupted only by shouts occasioned by the sighting of floating debris, boats, and sharks.

Around 1:00 the Cessna returned to the airstrip and then taxied down the runway for re-fueling. Danny had gathered up the children, grabbed a taxi, and now stood "at the ready" to begin his shift. I am grateful he had the guts to get in that airplane everyday in spite of his inevitable nausea and innate fear of small aircraft. I would have done the same for him. Maybe. Then again...

The only bright spot in Liz's hunt was her newfound affection for Antonio. Antonio would not be satisfied until I was found. A handsome, slender young man in his early 20's, he was resolute in his commitment to find the husband of the woman before him. A refreshing change of pace, the money was of little importance to him. His attitude instilled in Liz a sense of hope in what was a very bleak landscape. He also ran interference for the wide variety of Mexican officials whose good will meant the difference between flying or being grounded- his personality and a little grease, always grease.

A liaison to the American consulate's office was dispatched to the airport to intercept Liz as she disembarked from the airplane. Sent by John Desmond, she was an idiot whose official agenda remains a mystery, for her investigation consisted of interrogatories that alarmed Liz unnecessarily; inquiries that were of a personal nature such as "Does your husband have any scars, or identifiable bodily marks? How is your marriage? What was he wearing?" Liz mentioned that I was wearing a diamond ring which provoked a lengthy discourse about tourists who have met with foul play. Thievery on the seas was apparently commonplace. "I don't want to alarm you, she said, but pirating on the waters near Cozumel is abundant. The smart tourists avoid Cozumel and sail their boats near Playa del Carmen. It's much safer there. The banditos may have spotted him, helped him out of the water, saw the ring, robbed him, and pushed him overboard." Your husband's ring is valuable enough to cost him his life if he resisted. I'm sure Liz was very happy she stopped by.

Misery must come in pairs.

As Liz exited the cab on her return from the airport, she was accosted by a mean looking, goateed Mexican official. Perhaps from the Office of Health, he was sent by the Policia to deal with the American. Liz found him scary and full of himself. With his right arm drawn close and parallel to his body, his hand stroked his hairy chin in arrogant contemplation. He wrought devastation on Liz's fragile emotional state by remarking in an astounding array of disconnected thoughts, "It is stupid that you are conducting a search. It is fruitless to search. The fish will get him. You better have insurance. Getting the body back would be better. If there is no body you will have to wait 7 years. I have checked the hospital and morgue. Do you know what it takes to get a body out of here? It will have to be bagged by the funeral director..." He also verbalized a notion that "maybe this is big American plot. Maybe you came into this country without him. Maybe he never came and you are making it up." He droned on with details that Liz refused to hear.

His soliloquy was interrupted by the arrival of reporters from Cancun who had picked up the news from ship to ship transmissions and CB communications. They had come to interview Liz for a local news broadcast which would cover most of the coastal area, and the surrounding jungle as well. Liz and Danny's running speculation was that I had washed ashore on some remote beach, was hurt, or in a state of confusion, but that I could be found and returned to safety. The local broadcast could be a good thing.

On the second day and with a crushing sadness, Liz and Danny agreed that it was time to call the family. My sister Julia answered the telephone at my parents home. As usual, my Father was at work. Liz insisted that Julia turn the phone over to my mother so she could deliver the news of my disappearance directly to her. Access to a telephone line to the United States was spotty at best. She had been disconnected a number of times and was apprehensive that she might get cut off again.

"Ma, Dale is missing. He and Danny went out on jet-skis yesterday morning. Dale had trouble with his jet-ski and has been gone since then...it's a holiday weekend and I can't find any U.S. government officials. Danny is up in an airplane looking for him right now." My mother implored Liz to "please find him, please find him," all the while agonizing and crying over such horrifying news. Her son was missing. A mothers worst nightmare. She would not sleep. She would pray—and call my father with the news.

Turning the telephone over to Julia once again, Liz asked Julia to call our Senator and Congressman...and anyone who would listen.

Julia, to her credit, was a virtual calling machine, despite the fact that, initially, no one would listen. At first, a cold shoulder from all the media...except Channel 7 (ABC), the home of Bill Bonds and his professional equal—Cheryl Chodin.

The call to my father, in the meantime, would have a devastating effect on his already fragile constitution. My mother called his office and gave him the bad news. According to his secretary, he bowed his head, closed his eyes as if losing consciousness, and slumped in his chair. He then left for home, a beaten man. Ever the optimist, by nature strong willed and tough as nails—this he could not handle. Upon his arrival at home he disclosed to my mother that "If Dale is gone, it is the end for me."

There is nothing more heart wrenching than a recollection of my fathers reaction to the news, for my father passed away at 10:30 AM on July 27, 1997, the worst day of my life.

Understandably, it was a very short time before the entire family in Michigan, upstate New York, and New York City were briefed on the situation. EVERYONE swung into action. My sister-in-law Nancy from upstate New York began a round of calling to her congressman and every politician in the book. My cousin Lisa from SanDiego called the Coast Guard, and countless members of my immediate family in the Detroit area called every politician they could think of. A lot of noise.

News of "Dale is lost in the ocean" set afoot a flurry of plans at the home of Liz's mother and father, Joan and Bob. Liz is the oldest of 5 children and in order of oldest to youngest, Liz is the oldest followed by Robert, Daniel, John, and Joanne. One could not ask for a more loyal and warm family, each of them the product of a mother and father who lavished them with equal parts love and discipline. With the exception of Daniel who resides in Texas, Liz's other brothers Rob and John and sister Joanne live in New York.

The family assembled in short order and hatched plans to
lend support.

In the meantime, Liz set about to send Danny and the children back home. The three day Apple Tour vacation would be
over in the morning. With her husband gone for two full days,
she knew that it was time for Danny and the children to go home.
She insisted that their lives were to remain essentially unchanged.

Liz would not be coming home until I was rescued. She
would not leave me. The foundation of our relationship as husband and wife resides in the existence of a mutual work ethic. In
the matter of my rescue she possessed an inextinguishable will to
wage war. I fought for my life. She fought to save the life of our
family. We were engaged in the same war on different fronts. Her
courage was greater than mine, for her failure to find me alive
would condemn her to a life eclipsed by tragedy. I would have it
much easier. My life would have merely ended.

Liz needed her brother Daniel. Daniel, a deep sea diver,
was working on an oil rig off the coast of Louisiana. He was living
aboard the American Victory, a 165' support diving vessel. They
were 200 hundred miles out in the Gulf of Mexico. After numer-
ous attempts to reach the international telephone operator, Liz
was finally connected to his home in Freeport, Texas and spoke
with Daniel's wife Tara. Tara assured Liz that, although offshore,
he would be contacted. Liz gave instructions to get Daniel on an
airplane down to Cozumel. She would cover all the costs.

Liz's parents and her brother John were on their way from
New York to Michigan by car. They would care for the children

when they arrived back in Michigan.

Her brother Robert worked for Lockheed-Martin and was in California working at a radar installation site. He made arrangements to fly to Mexico on Monday.

Between Robert, a 6th degree blackbelt in Kung Fu, a guy who spent considerable time at remote radar/military outposts from the Arctic Circle to Saudi Arabia, and her brother Daniel, the REAL Diver Dan who risked his life in the water everyday—— Liz would truly have commandos at her side. A full day would pass before Daniel arrived.

With the advent of dusk on that 2nd day, Danny's shift came to a close as the single engine Cessna gently touched down on the runway and taxied to the hangar. Danny disembarked along with Kelly and Antonio. Head hung low, he caught a taxi and with bloodshot eyes, peered from the window of the car as it raced toward the hotel. He saw nothing. His thoughts were bound tightly within his mind, and he was completely blind to the surrounding tropical landscape.

Danny rejoined Liz and the children for dinner as darkness ensued. Returning to the hotel, Liz picked up a message from John Desmond. John had left his cellular phone number and asked that Liz return his call. He had been very busy but Liz's plight now had his full attention. He had begun to suspect that we were the victims of foul play. According to his reports, there was an emerging pattern of missing Americans, and the number of missing people seemed to be snowballing. He seriously weighed the wisdom of declaring this an 'international incident'.

He had been in contact with the U.S. Coastguard and asked them to conduct a search. Poised to launch an all out search, and prepared to send a ship from Florida, the Coastguard was rebuffed by the Mexican government. The government would not allow the coastguard to enter Mexican waters. The Mexican government was entirely uncooperative. The coastguard then offered to do a drift survey. The drift survey was created for the purpose of plotting my location to assist with the aerial search being conducted by Liz and Danny. The underlying assumption, albeit erroneous, was that I remained aboard the jet-ski. Calculating wind speed and water current, with a factor for the size and weight of the craft, they arrived at an estimate of my location.

It was their conclusion that I was drifting northeast in the general direction of Cuba. The U.S. Coastguard faxed the survey to the hotel. The hotel was pleased to accept the fax and added the fee to Liz's room charges. Such benevolence. I love those guys.

John Desmond, in his official role as a representative for the United States Embassy, made a formal request to the Mexican Government to intercede with the Cuban government on our behalf. The United States has not entertained diplomatic relations with Cuba since the Kennedy administration of the early '60's. As a result, Mr. Desmond was restrained from communicating any pleadings directly to the Cuban government.

At Mr. Desmond's request, officials of the Mexican government contacted the Cuban government. The Cuban diplomats declined all requests for assistance. I was an American. They would offer assistance to Mexicans only.

Concurrently, officials from the Mexican navy advised Mr. Desmond that they would be calling off the search on Monday morning. They were quoted as remarking that "By that time, he would be eaten by sharks, or dead anyway." Their postscript aside, John Desmond was perplexed with their stated position. They had never looked anyway. Liz responded to the news by uttering, "No way in hell. He's not dead. He's hurting and he may be at the end of his rope, but he's NOT DEAD. He won't give up because of the kids."

Liz thanked John Desmond for his help.

And, indeed, up to that point, 2 days after I had disappeared, Liz remained steadfast in her belief that I was alive, but she was now starting to doubt.

She muttered to herself, "It has been much too long." With those words, Liz's confidence in my ability to survive whatever ordeal I was faced with began to wane. More importantly, her faith in her own power to 'will me' to safety began to crumble.

Later that evening, a pair of nurses from Houston offered Liz some sleeping pills to get her through the night. She refused. She insisted on remaining alert for me and the children. Liz packed the suitcases for the early morning departure as Danny wrestled with Joey and Stefanie. They hunkered down for the second successive night, awaiting the arrival of first light.

Sometime in the middle of the night, a single sheet of paper was slipped quietly under the door. It was the final check-out slip. Two precious little children, not a care in the world, their mouths wide open, drooling contentedly, their mother distraught and sleeping in fits beside them, were being thrown out. The Apple Tours vacation was over.

The children were going home anyway, but Liz would not tolerate such reprehensible behavior. It's called 'life according to Liz' and she would not be tossed about like excess chattel. The first morning light appeared faintly at the edges of the curtained window beside her bed beckoning her to awaken and seize another day. Sleep had come in fits and starts, exhaustion at the fore. She noticed the paper on the floor as she walked to the bathroom. In addition to the sense of sight, sound, touch, feel, and taste, New Yorkers are also born with the sense of cynicism. It would be reasonable to conclude that Liz, a true New Yorker, would not be surprised by anything. Yet, she was shocked by the callous attitude of the Fiesta Americana hotel. "It is much too early for this" she remarked to herself.

She dressed for the first battle of the day.

Liz emerged from the elevator on this, the third day of her search, and strode boldly toward the registration desk, galvanized by the audacity of the hotel to ask that she leave. She spoke to a young Mexican woman behind the desk who spoke only Spanish and found her to be of no assistance. In the four days since our arrival, the manager had never shown his face. Screaming at the top of her lungs, Liz demanded to see the Manager. She would be denied no longer. A busload of arriving guests began to fill the lobby as she continued her tirade, intent upon creating a scene and embarrassing the manager into granting her an audience.

'Mr. Rico Suave', a fitting acronym for the manager, whose

name Liz cannot remember, finally came out of his office. He was in his 30's, with black slicked back hair, black eyes, white crisp shirt and tie, dress slacks, and well defined muscles. He was not short, not exceedingly tall, and not nice. In any other situation, he may have projected perhaps a disarming aloofness, a certain elegance that women may have found enchanting or at least, garnered a second look. In this case, Liz found him to be arrogant and profoundly ignorant.

He insisted that Liz leave, pointing out that "all the rooms are booked. We have no rooms. Your Apple Tour is over." An agent from a rental car company, seated at a table near the front desk, came to Liz's defense and told the manager to leave her alone. Liz was grateful for his kind gesture, but she didn't need his help. She had her own advice for the manager, or for that matter, anyone else in shouting range.

Liz's rage was overwhelming, her eyes like lasers, points of light burning into the managers fixed glare as she told him exactly how it was going to go.

"This is the last place where my husband saw me. This is where I will be when he comes back. I am going to the airport to send my children home and I am going back up in the air to search for him. I am taking my key and when I come back I am going to my room. My luggage better be there when I return. I will tell you when I'm checking out. You will not tell me."

Her words were powerful and very effective. She turned about and headed for her room to gather the children and Danny for their return to the United States of America, home.

She was not bothered by the hotel management again.

With the Coastguard grid chart in hand, Liz, Danny, Stefanie, Joey, Kelly and Eduardo from the diveshop headed for the airport. Antonio the pilot would meet Liz, Kelly and Eduardo.

With a heavy heart, Liz assured Danny that none of this was his fault. He was not to feel guilty. She did not hold him responsible. "Take the kids and go. Now I have to kick butt."

Poor Danny. The whole story was in his eyes, vacant and lifeless. He felt responsible. He knew I was dead. Without me, life was going to be very different. Liz drew the children to her breast and alternately kissed their heads, tears in her eyes, wondering when she would see them next for she would not leave until I was found, alive or dead. Releasing them from her embrace and into Danny's care, he scooped them up and boarded the plane.

Liz turned to Kelley and declared that she wanted the airplane until Friday. Kelley, the gentle soul she is, remarked, "Liz, whatever you want. When you feel you have done the best you can, you tell me." In her mind, unspoken, Kelley knew that I was dead. She had experience. Her husbands body had never been recovered.

With the departure of the commercial airliner that held her family and a full load of American tourists, Liz and company met to discuss strategy. After two full days of flying by the seat of their pants, searching instinctively, and at altitudes that were restricted by Mexican law, the grid chart presented realistic opportunities. To fully integrate the grid chart into an intelligent search, it was necessary to fly much lower, and that presented bureaucratic difficulties— having to deal with Mexican officials again. This time,

Antonio the pilot was dispatched to deal with the next bureacrat. That official came in the form of a man seated at a creaky wooden chair in a sparsely furnished old office with a ceiling fan for air-conditioning. He looked much older than his 60's. He also had greasy slicked back hair. His shirt buttons strained to be free of his bloated stomach, as he chewed on a short, wet cigar. A dog-eared notebook lay upon the desk before him and was the only sign of official government documentation. He acknowledged the polite young man who stood before him with an economy of effort by uttering "Permisso?" A short dialogue in Spanish between Antonio and the official ensued, at the end of which Liz was required to pay a small fee. More grease.

The little airplane lifted off the runway in the direction of the Yucatan peninsula to the north. From there they would fly east toward Cuba in both a zig zag and grid pattern. With permit in hand they flew as low as 100 feet from the surface of the water. As they approached Cuba, Antonio warned Liz that he could not guarantee her safety in Cuban airspace. His plane would be ticketed and as an American, she would surely be held prisoner.

They turned back.

They returned for re-fueling mid-day and then resumed their search until 5:00. Three full days of an intensive search yielded nothing. Friday, Saturday, and Sunday and all they had seen were a lot of nice fish, an occasional boat, garbage, and sharks.

Liz returned to the Hotel and the privacy of her room. As expected, the luggage had not been touched. All alone and sore to the point of exhaustion from the constant jostling of the aircraft, she lay across the bed and began to cry. She was at her wits end and all alone in the world.

Daniel, her brother, was scheduled to arrive around 8:00 in the evening. Daniel's employer, American Oilfield Divers, Inc. and Unocal, in a gesture of goodwill toward one of their own, and for which I remain eternally grateful, flew Daniel in a helicopter from the oil rig upon which he was working, to the nearest airport. Being ferried by helicopter was highly unusual. The divers were transported by ship only and lived and worked on the platform for periods ranging from a few weeks to a month or longer. Commuting was not an option. It seems that the entire company from Louisiana to Texas rallied in their support. From the Operations manager in Lafayette, Louisiana who made the travel arrangements and paid for the tickets to Mexico with company money, to the driver from New Orleans Operations who picked Daniel up at the heli-pad and gave him spending money, the company gave their all. Daniel had thrown a fresh change of clothes and his deep sea gear in a large canvas bag and sprinted toward the sound of chopper blades. From the flight deck above, the helicopter blades whirred with a deafening volume. He was whisked to the airport in Louisiana where he picked up a commercial flight to Cancun, and from there, a flight to the island of Cozumel.

As the hour of his arrival approached, Liz cleaned up, left her room, and lay upon a wicker lounge chair in the lobby. She focused her attention on all the people exiting the cars and busses that pulled into the hotel portico. Liz anxiously anticipated the safety of her brother's embrace.

Daniel did arrive shortly thereafter. A man of quiet strength, one not given to displays of false bravado, he gently hugged his sister and for the moment, however brief, restored her sense of well-being. He was shocked at her condition, finding her pale and cool to the touch, her skin pliable and colorless.

Liz and Daniel returned to her room, stowed his luggage, and did a thorough run-thru of events. It remains unclear as to the value of bringing his diving gear other than to suggest that Daniel would do anything his sister asked of him. It was a big ocean and he was prepared to dive anywhere she asked.

For the time being, all they could do was wait until morning.

At 1:00 AM on Monday morning, the fourth day of my disappearance, with Daniel diligently attempting to calm his sister and usher her back to good health, the telephone began to ring. Now in charge, and prepared to endure the worst, Daniel picked up the receiver. It was John Desmond. Briefed earlier by Liz, Daniel knew who John Desmond was and asked Mr. Desmond to please discuss his business with him. John politely declined, insisting that he speak directly to Mrs. Chimenti. Daniel turned his eyes to Liz, assumed the worst, and uttered the hardest words he had ever spoken by saying "I'm sorry Liz." He handed her the telephone, convinced beyond a doubt that Mr. Desmond was calling to inform Liz of my death. It could be nothing else. He was devastated.

"Mrs. Chimenti, your husband is alive!" A German freighter picked him up early Sunday evening. I understand he is in stable condition and headed for Port Everglades Florida."

T H E   S E C O N D   L I F E

Knowing Liz as I do, I can speculate on her reaction to the good news. The initial, unalloyed joy she experienced must have given way to a flurry of activity. Energized, Liz would now focus her attention to the matter of orchestrating our re-union and getting everyone home safe and sound. With a prodigious capacity for work, Liz would move mountains if they were in the way. And so it was in the early morning hours of the happiest day of her life, that her husband, to whom she was devoted, was, unbelievably, alive. She would devote all her attention to my rehabilitation. With my characteristic independence, not unlike her own, I would resist.

Liz and her brother Daniel finally fell asleep around 2:30 in the morning, arose at 5:30, packed their bags, and headed to the airport for an Aero Mexico flight to Miami. With only a change of underwear, a T-shirt, and toothbrush in her purse, they arrived in Miami. Apple Tours had agreed to route her luggage to Detroit. They rented a car at the airport and drove to Ft. Lauderdale where they eagerly awaited my arrival. The Florida coastline was lined with hotels one after the other. Liz would not hear of it. She was convinced that the last thing I wanted to see was more water. A room overlooking the ocean, in her estimation, would not be acceptable. They found a comfortable inland hotel and drove to the port, expecting my arrival aboard ship. It would be one more day before we docked.

S . S . A L M A N I A

Returning to my own experience aboard ship and wasting no time, the S.S. Almania resumed her westerly heading in the direction of the United States the moment I was safely aboard. By the time Liz and Daniel were informed of my rescue and made preparations for their trip to Miami, we had been underway for over 8 hours. It would not be long before we rounded Key West and entered the Atlantic Ocean and the trip north along the Florida coast. I remained in the womb for two days. I miss that ship and wish I could go back. The wall adjacent to my bunk was warm to the touch and transmitted the vibration of the engines, deep within the bowels of the ship, to my body. Powerful and reassuring, the ship rocked me to sleep and held me safely in its arms.

The business of shipping, unlike my own experience as a brief but welcome passenger, must be much different for those whose lives are spent at sea. I recognized, very quickly, the existence of a two class system. The officers were predominantly German and Russian while the crew was Phillipino. The Phillipino crewmen attended to the needs of the officers and ate their meals in separate adjacent quarters. The Captain invited me to join him and the other officers for dinner and assisted me to a chair in the anteroom of his private quarters where we were joined by the Chief Engineer and a few other officers. A casual setting, and not the least bit formal, it was, nonetheless, very different from the crew dining area that adjoined it. I was struck by the segregated nature of the two groups and felt uncomfortable that I, an uninvited guest, was being treated better than the crewmen. I had no intention of eating, as I could not handle solid food, but felt that my presence violated some precept of fundamental human decency. These same men who helped me were somehow not good enough to dine with the rest of us. In defense of the Officers, perhaps my interpretation was a bit too circumspect and sorely ignorant in the ways of military or nautical social systems. The fact was, I felt ungrateful and decided to acknowledge these men by joining them as they ate. Thanking Captain Richter for his hospitality, I informed him that I desired to introduce myself to some of the men, and excused myself from the table. I entered their dining room and was received like a visiting dignitary. The men were consumed with joy that I had actually joined them. Their dining area was nothing more than a working kitchen with small picnic table type wood platforms where the men sat in pairs or alone, consuming bowls of food. Their diet consisted mainly of rice and fish. I graciously accepted their offer of a bowl of rice and decided they didn't have it bad after all. The officers were eating red meat and potatoes. It didn't take long to figure out who had clogged arteries and who didn't. I was satisfied that I had demonstrated my respect for their humanity. They later assisted me to the stern of the ship where I observed them fishing without fishing poles. With only a hook and fishing line, they threw the line out by hand and caught fish. Later, I asked Captain Richter why the men did not use fishing poles. He told me that they were too expensive. I wondered, sadly, what their annual income might have been, and seriously considered sending them all fishing poles.

Unconsciously, I was drawn to the pilot house and spent as much time as my frail condition would allow, sitting on the cushioned platform, the deck of the ship layed out before me and as long as a football field, surrounded by ocean for as far as one could see. I couldn't believe I was out of the water. Neither could Captain Richter. I asked him about all those hotels I saw in the distance. He replied, solemnly, that there were no hotels. I saw only the horizon. Handing me the binoculars, he insisted I look at the water before us and the horizon beyond. "What do you see?" Not waiting for a response, he offered, "You see nothing, only the horizon. There are no hotels. You would never be saved. A man cannot be seen even 100 yards from here."

I reflected on the night from hell when I had reached down with my feet to touch bottom, convinced beyond a doubt that I was in shallow water. "Captain Richter, I swore that I could almost touch bottom a few nights ago. Was that possible?" His answer left me in shock.

"My friend, that water is 3,000 feet deep."

I was terrified.

He left me to ponder the gravity of his words and the mag-

nitude of my rescue. He was both amused and in awe for I had
won a fight that couldn't be won.

Captain Richter walked to the chart table, removed the various plotting instruments from the surface of the chart that lay
upon its surface and stamped its surface with the insignia of the
SS Almania. He stuffed it into a plain brown envelope. He towered above me with an outstretched hand and with dramatic
flourish, handed me the envelope and said "Happy Birthday." He
had plotted my pick-up point on the navigational chart. 86/22
22/30. In his eyes, my place of birth, my second life.

The sight of the U.S. coastline stimulated the most provoca-
tive moment of my entire experience. I was both fascinated and
awed by the enormity of the buildings that towered high above
the earth and stretched into perpetuity. I had never been on a
ship in the ocean. I had never seen how the other side lived. I
never expected to see our country again. I really was alive, pricked
awake by the sight of land and, at least temporarily, jolted out of
my state of circumspection, and awarded with a sight to behold. I
pressed the binoculars to my eyes for hours. I couldn't get enough.
I was taken by the sight of my country. I said aloud, "The United
States of America." I was proud to return home. Even though I
had never seen the coastline before, and despite the fact that the
view was entirely foreign to me, I just knew that it was home.

I had been aboard the MS Almania for a full day as we prepared to drop anchor off the coast of Ft. Lauderdale, Florida in
Port Everglades. It is my recollection that the large ships refrain
from entering the Port at night, opting for the safety of daylight

to negotiate the myriad channels leading to a final berth. The Coast Guard was well aware of my presence aboard ship and had been anticipating my arrival. Liz and Daniel had arrived earlier that day and were disappointed that we had not yet arrived. She kept in close contact with the Coast Guard and encouraged them to rendezvous with the ship and pick me up as soon as we were in the area, intent upon whisking me to the hospital for immediate medical attention.

The Coast Guard did make contact with the ship to inquire of my medical status and determine if I was fit to board a small rescue boat for the ride to the mainland. For the second time in two days, I was asked if I could climb a jacobs ladder. The Coast Guard appeared overly anxious that I come ashore. I really did not want to leave and questioned Captain Richter in the matter of my right to stay aboard until we docked the next day. It was abundantly clear that I was in no position to climb a rope ladder and I just wanted to go back to my room. The Coast Guard, as I learned later, had only reacted in response to Liz's persistent requests to get me ashore. The Captain assented to my wish to remain a stowaway for one more night.

It was also interesting to learn that all ships entering a United States port must relinquish all control of the ship to U.S. personnel who motor out to the various ships and, in lay terms, drive them in. A single 'pilot' would normally board ship. In my case, we were treated to a small contingent of pilots who were so excited to meet me. Three pilots were dispatched to our ship for the ride in. I sat on my little perch in the pilot house aboard ship as they entered the room. I grasped the edge of my seat and stood up as they walked single file across the room to greet me. I felt unworthy of their praise. The first pilot stood at attention, and with a bearing more suitable to royalty, saluted me. He then shook my hand and said that I was a hero. The other men shook my hand and enthusiastically offered their congratulations and pleasure at having met me. Heady stuff for sure, but I was never a hero. Not then. Not now.

With the pilots at the controls, we began our approach to the Port. Surely a candidate for a History channel documentary, the port was awash in an infinite number of new and old ships of every imaginable size and shape and condition. Rusting old hulks of W.W.II vintage navy ships, carcasses of old fishing boats long since abandoned, huge tankers and more. Against the backdrop of these boats stood the gleaming chrome magnificence of the U.S. Coastguard ship. The men wore crisply pressed uniforms, and were busy maintaining its viral splendor.

Quietly, and with no fanfare, we arrived at the designated dock. High above stood an immense steel frame that supported a winch mounted on a track that ran for hundreds of feet across the concrete receiving area. I could only imagine scores of men and their hi-lo's scurrying about moving the containers being unloaded from the ships, for the dock was eerily abandoned that day. It was a Monday, but we assumed all was quiet because it was President's Day, a legal holiday. The only sign of life was a reporter from ABC and his cameraman. Liz was nowhere in sight.

An agent of the U.S. Immigration office, a representative of the U.S. Coast Guard, and a Customs agent came aboard to question me. Straightforward and to the point, they nonetheless congratulated me, and proceeded with the business of protecting American interests, each of the agents asking me a series of questions relevant to their individual occupational duties. I told them that I just couldn't remember who had won the World Series the prior year, or any year for that matter. Good thing they were amused.

It was Tuesday morning, 5 days after Danny and I had sped from shore on our jet-skis and I was about to touch the terra firma— in a big way.

O N L Y   I N   A M E R I C A

Andy Warhol was fundamentally correct when he said everyone would have 15 minutes of fame. In my case, the appearance of a lone reporter and cameraman at the dock gave-way to a whirlwind of interest from the media that has lasted for years.

The aftermath of my experience at sea has proven to be ever as interesting and in some respects, even more challenging than the life and death ordeal which I faced in the ocean. The story of my will to live and Liz's singular devotion to my rescue gave birth to a veritable encyclopedia of events which took on a life of its own— and which I trust the reader will find equally fascinating.

As to my tenure aboard ship, I wondered why Liz was not at the dock to meet me upon our arrival and I was hesitant to disembark and talk to the reporter. The Captain told me that the reporter was there to interview me. A representative of the shipping line that owned the MS Almania boarded the ship to greet me and offer his congratulations. I extended my sincerest appreciation for their hospitality. The government agents had concluded their questioning and released me as well. I no longer had any business aboard ship. It was time to go. Captain Richter said to "keep the clothes" and bade me good-bye, his beautiful wife at my side as I grasped the railing at the top of a flight of steps and made my way, slowly, to the gang plank and off the ship.

The reporter introduced himself and thrust a microphone in my face as the cameraman recorded our conversation. In the space of a few minutes, a van crossed the tarmac at an accelerated clip and came to an abrupt stop within 20 feet of us. The passenger door flew open and my wife emerged running to me and yelling my name, her arms wide open, beseeching me to hold her. She wanted proof I was alive. It was all over. I had made it. I was back and boy was she looking good. Quite the babe. Daniel stood back and watched. I saw in his eyes the look of one who couldn't believe what he was witnessing. His eyes said, "this is one tough and very lucky man. My sister will be okay now."

I love my brother in laws. It was clearly mutual. Liz and I hugged as she repeated over and over, "I knew you wouldn't die, I knew you weren't dead. They wouldn't listen to me. I told them you were too mean to die."

We concluded the interview and headed for the hospital. I wasn't feeling very well.

The rest is history, as they say, for I have since accumulated hours of television footage beginning with the moment I set foot on that pier in Port Everglades, Florida.

Chuck Malkus. For some reason, I can't get rid of that name. It is one of the few names that seems to linger in my consciousness for no apparent reason, perhaps its sound, a typical Midwestern American name, plain, unimaginative, boring; bereft of the multi-syllabic, rich, historied sounds of Latin names that roll off the tongue. Maybe it was the garish manner in which he introduced himself as the public relations representative for Broward General Hospital, offering a big handshake and even wider grin as he proceeded to invade my world with instructions on how we were going to handle the press. "Press?" I asked. I thought we already did that.

"Mr. Chimenti, we can have them interview you in this room individually or we can move to a special area where you can submit to their questions all at one time."

"How many are there?" a quizzical look on my face.

"There is a crowd of them. There are reporters from all the local papers, there are film crews from all the television networks, and there are producers from Inside Edition, the television show."

I laughed. "You've got to be kidding. What for?"

"They are here to see you. You have an incredible story to tell. I wouldn't be surprised if you get movie offers."

Liz and I agreed that one all inclusive interview would be best. With an IV in my arm, the nurses had administered a drip that restored my sense of balance and I felt solid. I slid out of bed into a wheelchair, and with Daniel driving, Liz, CHUCK, and I left for Hollywood, figuratively speaking.

"Wow" was my reaction. A room the size of two large classrooms was filled with reporters, journalists, and cameramen; a fraternity of people chatting aimlessly as we entered the room. A discernible quiet rippled across the room as we made our way to a table adorned with microphones. The floor was strewn with miles of wire crisscrossing its surface. We submitted to their polite questioning. I felt obligated to deliver interesting answers to their questions. They had, after all, come all this way to see me. I felt responsible.

I managed to mention American Express and their role in assisting Liz by way of the airplane rental. American Express was famous for running ads on the many different ways their cardholders used their cards. This was perfect. Maybe they were watching.

At the conclusion of the media coverage, Chuck whispered in my ear that producers from Inside Edition were waiting in another room down the hall and "would we talk to them?" I agreed. Although polite, Liz considered the press an invasion of our privacy. Her maternal instincts in full bloom, she focused on protecting me. Given the choice, Liz would have ignored the media altogether. My instincts? SHOW ME THE MONEY. I've been in business for too long not to look for an angle. I pondered the possibilities. How could I increase the gross revenues in my business? Practically speaking, there was no way. I was in the wholesale equipment business. I did not sell to the general public. As to the lingerie stores, women, or men for that matter, were not about to buy more underwear as a result of my newfound fame.

Chuck led us to our interview with Inside Edition, coursing down the hallways, eliciting stares from the staff and patients lining the halls. I felt very uncomfortable, not knowing whether they were staring at my face that looked like it had been bobbing for french fries or because I was suddenly famous. Either reason was cause for discomfort.

We found ourselves face to face with a producer in his mid 20's and a smart-ass. Harmless, but a smart-ass nonetheless. A heavy woolen coat was draped over the chair in front of him. I said to him, "This is Florida, why do you have a winter coat? He responded impatiently, "I just flew in from New York. Why else would I have a winter coat?"

I was truly perplexed. "Why did you fly in from New York? Why are you here?"

"We came to see you." With a stupified look on my face, I asked him, "What could you possibly find interesting about my story that you would actually go through the trouble and expense of flying in from New York?"

He leaned forward in his chair and looked me straight in the eye. He said, "we are tired of the blood and gore. In our business we see carnage every day. Your story has a happy ending. You lived! You were lost at sea and lived to tell about it. We were thrilled to come down here."

I understood.

With our Florida interview captured on film and utilizing stock footage from their film archive, Inside Edition completed their piece. Our story was aired on their nightly broadcast shortly thereafter. It was re-aired 4 more times over the following 2 years. Hopefully, a legacy to my grandchildren, should I someday be so lucky. If I am ever in a wheelchair, drooling into a cup, they can pull out those VHS videotapes from the dark ages, and ponder the imponderable; that once, a very very long time ago, their grizzened old grandfather did something very cool.

In the meantime, my stay at Broward General hospital was short lived. I felt so good from the electrolytes or whatever they were pumping directly into my veins that I insisted on leaving immediately, against their recommendation. Being foolish was my right. They also sent a psychiatrist for a quick looksee and then released me. The decision to leave the hospital was pure folly. I fell into a state of dizziness and was severely out of sorts shortly after the IV was removed.

We ducked out through a seldom used exit and headed for the hotel for the night. Our flight left in the morning for Detroit Metropolitan Airport. I wanted to see my children as soon as possible.

Liz intuitively anticipated the overwhelming response to our story by the media and concerned for my privacy, she registered, earlier, under her maiden name and insisted to the hotel staff that, if asked, they deny knowledge of our status as hotel guests. For the most part, they complied with her wishes. However, messages were piling up at the desk from newspaper reporters around the country. Given the time I had spent with all the other TV and print media, I felt obligated to support my hometown newspaper. From our room at the hotel, I returned a call from Cecil Angel of the Detroit Free Press. Cecil was a pleasure to speak with, and although Seth Borenstein from the Sun-Sentinel was not a Michigan reporter, I acknowledged his request for a personal interview also. He was one of the reporters at the hospital and I liked him. By and large, most of the reporters with whom we conducted the hospital interview were there for themselves. They struck me as pretentious, not the least bit endearing, and really not interested in me. I was there to narrate a story. All done? Bye bye, now. Gotta go. On the other hand, Seth seemed to have a heart.

The competitive nature of the news business became quite clear in the form of a TV station manager by the name of Mort Meisner from the CBS affiliate in Detroit. Mort made repeated attempts to contact us at the hospital and our hotel. He was bold enough to suggest to Liz, who ran interference against all comers, that we were old high school buddies and therefore he should have a chance to talk with me. Actually, we had gone to the same high school and I did recall attending a class with him. I also vaguely recalled him sitting near the back with some other guy and being completely obnoxious—one of those guys who had a mouth and ego to match. I also could not recall a time when he would lower his standards to extend even a personal greeting. I should have rewarded his resourcefulness, instead I looked up at Liz, smiled, and said, "F— him." It was beautiful. Paybacks are great. Liz liked it too.

Daniel left on a flight to Houston that same evening. Liz was afraid to leave me while she dropped him off at the airport. I couldn't blame her. She hoped I wouldn't get into any trouble while she was gone. She prayed for handcuffs. We spent the night at the hotel and left for the airport first thing in the morning. With Liz pushing me in a wheel chair, we proceeded through the terminal to our gate. To my horror, people came up to us asking for my autograph. It was not a crowd, but people recognized me from Television.

"Are you that guy on TV? Are you the hero?"

I never harbored the illusion, in my entire life, that I would accomplish anything that would result in anyone asking for my autograph. Nothing had altered that fact. I didn't feel worthy to affix my signature to their papers. I was embarrassed. I had accomplished nothing that qualified for preferential status outside of dragging my sorry butt out of the drink, and that wasn't good enough. Yet, how could I refuse a simple accommodation? Refusal would effect even more attention and breed resentment. To the first person who handed me their pen and paper, I offered with great humility, "Sir, I am not a hero. I do not feel worthy to give you my autograph. If I had saved 100 children from a burning building, I would be a hero. I did not do that."

He would hear nothing of it. One of life's lessons, I learned that I could not alter his perception of who or what I represented. It was not my place to decide if my autograph had value to him. I signed his chit...and a few others.

It was time to go home.

Northwest Airlines, benevolent by nature, and in a magnificent gesture of goodwill, were kind enough to sell us one- way tickets to Detroit's Metropolitan Airport for the princely sum of $700.00 each, one way. Talk about predators. I fared better with real sharks.

You'd think we were movie stars. We exited the airplane in Detroit and were greeted by a crowd of hundreds. The lights were blinding. I was overwhelmed by the crowd of reporters and movie cameras and banks of lights. I raised my hand to my eyes to shield them from the glare and to see ahead. My mother and father, Danny, and my Aunt Isabelle stepped forward to welcome me home. I hugged my dad and told him, with a mixture of pride and pain, that I made it. Choked up, I uttered "I made it Dad." I always sought his approval. His face said it all.

My mother hugged me and said I looked awful. Gee, thanks ma. She also said, "no more vacations for you!" A surreptitious grin, I looked at Danny and yelled, "Okay Ma, I'll never go on vacation again." Yea right.

Danny gave me a hug. With simple facial expressions, we were back in synch, an unspoken mutual exchange that said, "lights!, camera!, action! This is way too cool. Can you believe this? Who would of ever thunk?" Being true opportunists, with the cameras rolling, I said, "On our next vacation, we're going to Disney World!" Opportunists in plural because my words mirrored Danny's thoughts. He was thinking the same thing. We laughed heartily at the same time. Maybe the Disney people were watching. It was just the perfect moment to say it and way too funny. Danny and I have a hard time being serious about anything. Sarcasm 'R Us.

Along with our immediate family, Liz and I were seated on an electric transport. It was one of those carts where we mere common folk cast jealous glances at the anointed few who are exempt from a very long walk. With reporters jostling for position, amidst a frenzy of questions, and with microphones thrust in our faces, we were whisked away to another part of the airport. My mother had agreed to grant WXYZ channel 7 a private and exclusive interview.

I swung my legs out from the cart, and with help from Liz, was escorted to a diminutive lady with a microphone in her hand. She looked familiar and she was crying. She also gave me a hug. She was a TV newsperson. I was confused. I thought to myself, "Why is she crying? She is a newsreporter. Aren't they all cold and heartless? Besides, she doesn't even know me." I glanced at my mother in search of an answer. With few words my mother explained that this was Cheryl Chodin, Bill Bond's associate, and she was our friend. Indeed she was. Cheryl was genuinely happy for me and my family. She had spent a long time in my parents home. She was also a professional. The first to arrive on the scene at my parents home, Cheryl had politely, but very aggressively turned down the inquiries of all the reporters who, subsequently, knocked on my parents door. Mort Meisner, from the CBS affiliate, got his butt kicked again. Cheryl answered the door by pulling it open just enough to speak through the crack. Cheryl responded to all comers with "I'm handling it." Good for her. A very tough lady with a heart of gold.

Both Cheryl and Mike Holfield fed live camera and news reports to Bill Bonds for the midday, 6 and 11:00 news every day for over a week. I was thrilled to be the recipient of Bills emotional largesse. Equal parts virulent and benevolent, Bill Bonds was either friend or foe, never lacking an opinion, and despite widely publicized personal tragedies, he was well respected. He made me feel like a man. He confirmed all that I had worked so hard for. At the conclusion of one nights report, he leaned back in his chair, and with sincere reflection, a personal aside, he looked into the camera and said, "That is one tough dude."

Initially, I was rather detached from the roller coaster of emotions that my family and friends must have experienced. I thought nothing of it. It did not occur to me that everyone had experienced the absolute worst news followed in short order by great news. They experienced the lowest of lows to the highest of highs. All I knew was that I had won. "What's everyone getting excited about?" I did not stop to consider the effect that my disappearance would have upon everyone, but I saw it in my father's eyes. At my mothers suggestion, my father arranged for us to be transported from the airport to our home by limousine. At the conclusion of our interview with Cheryl Chodin, my mother and father, Liz, Danny and I made our way in the frigid winter air to the limo. I was so thankful for the limousine as I was much too sick to endure the trip home in a confined space. I was seated on a side bench with my mother and father sitting in the proverbial 'bride and groom' seats. I rested my head on the seat back, too tired to hold my head up. I turned my eyes in the direction of my father as we pulled away from the curb.

My father was crying. I had never seen my father cry in my entire life. I was so immediately regretful that I had caused him so much pain. I was devoted to my father. I held my father blameless in the matter of what he coulda, shoulda, woulda done as my father while I was growing up. Too many children of my generation held their parents responsible for everything wrong with their own lives. Not me. I looked upon my father with the words of

Jackie Gleason upon my lips. He was the greatest. I guess my experience did have consequence in the lives of others. I hoped the joy of getting his son back would mitigate the pain my father had endured.

We arrived in Troy, a bitter cold winter evening, to the handshakes of a few hardy neighbors who waited in the driveway huddled against the biting wind. A camera crew from the ABC news affiliate and Inside Edition also awaited our arrival. After pulling into the driveway and stepping out of the car, and in one of life's uncomfortable moments, the limo driver, a young man in perhaps his mid 20's, came to me and shook my hand. With formal bow of the head and with deep personal conviction, he said that it was an honor to meet me. All of that with my father standing next to me. I couldn't imagine "feeling honored" with my father standing next to me. The driver also said that he was scheduled to pick up Rod Stewart's mother and had chosen to pick me up instead. That I understood. She probably sang worse than her son, if that were possible.

Danny took care of the tip.

The glass storm door was caked with ice and frost, a clue that many members of my family had graced our home with their presence, eager to celebrate our return; indeed, my aunts and uncles, cousins, and of course, Liz's mother who had diligently prepared food for all.

Most important of all were my children. I lived to see them again. I entered the house and there stood Stefanie and Joey. On that day I was the happiest guy in the universe. All the pain and anguish was worth it. I won the game.

"Hey Joey, how was your vacation?" He was a trifle young to understand the humor behind the question. I thought it was funny.

I visited with the family as much as my condition would allow. I felt obligated to be a gracious host and at least talk to everyone. I should have recognized that I was the guest. I was too weak to sit and my voice was no more than a hoarse whisper. I was also much too out of sorts to engage in conversation. We conducted more on-camera interviews. Liz was done with those guys. She had had enough.

With the last departing guest, our house became our home once again. The trip from hell had officially ended.

In 70's parlance, however, the beat goes on...the story never ending. The telephone rang constantly, articles continued to appear in numerous papers and magazines, and the onslaught of requests for interviews continued unabated.

In the meantime, I began a slow return to health. I was much sicker than I believed myself to be. I felt very dizzy and unsteady on my feet, very sluggish, and out of sorts. Walking was like swimming, each step a struggle to move forward. I had left the hospital too soon. What a dummy. I should have stayed at Broward General for awhile. Liz decided that I needed to be re-admitted to the local hospital. I was much too weak to dispute her decision. Off we went to Beaumont Hospital.

My first venture out of the house after returning home from the hospital in Michigan was an appearance at our Macomb County lingerie store. We were greeted with cheers and tears by

all our employees. The girls (models) all lined up to give me hugs.
Life could be much worse. They were so happy to have us back.
We were very fair and honest employers and fortunately, com-
manded their respect. I was particularly moved by Courtney.
Courtney was a strikingly beautiful woman. Sarcastic by nature,
arrogant to the bone, she had a lightening quick and acerbic wit.
We enjoyed each others company as we commonly engaged in a
harmless war of words, sparring playfully. I was equal to the task.
On that particular day, she displayed a depth of emotion I would
never have expected. An Ice woman no more. She put her arms
around me and sobbed tears of relief. She held me and cried. I
was so very moved. I had brought out the best in her, and we
really were friends. Interestingly enough, Courtney's boyfriend,
who she later married, is Chris Campbell, longtime bass player
for the Bob Seger Silver Bullet Band. Sometime later, Chris and
Courtney threw a welcome home party for Liz and I at Legends
nightclub in downtown Detroit. Part owner of Legends, Chris set
aside the entire upper floor for our party. All my friends were
invited, along with many members of my family, all the employees of AFI and It's Our Pleasure, my friends Bill, Rose and Shannon
Stacey (Pilat) from the health club, the Mayor of Troy and a host
of significant others.

   In particular, our friends Stuart and Andrea Rubin had
graced us by making the pilgrimage to downtown Detroit. Both
Liz and I, at various times, and under completely separate and
distinct circumstances, had been involved with Stu and Andrea in
business. From a chance business relationship, we had developed

a mutual respect and deep abiding friendship for each other.
Andrea and Stu are very creative people. Andrea is one of the
brightest people I have ever met. In fact, she is brilliant. Very
perceptive, she possesses what I call '3 dimensional' thinking,
capable of interpreting abstract intellectual concepts in a manner analogous to examining an object held in the hand, turning
it over and describing it from all sides, her thoughts delivered in
rapid succession; like pulling the trigger. Stu, a very loving individual, a conscientious chiropractor and frustrated screen writer,
pulled a list of Dale jokes from his suit pocket. Stu and Andrea
had prepared a Stupid Joke List. Very gutsy, considering the circumstance. There were a lot of people in the room whose last
names ended in a vowel and whose idea of a feast included a
salami sandwich with a chunk of cheese that reeked of old socks.
It was not a good room for a couple of Jewish kids. Maybe I
wouldn't like those jokes...

In an humorous attempt to mock the purple bathing suit
that I had worn on my head during the journey at sea, Liz and the
girls had decided that the party at Legends would have a purple
theme. They all wore purple dresses. I was escorted to the dance
floor on the main level by all the girls. It was a Saturday night and
the main floor was packed. To the incredulous stares of all, we
took to the floor. The girls propped me up and danced with only
me. Fifteen or more absolutely stunning, knock down gorgeous
women all dancing exclusively with me. At one point, I excused
myself to use the bathroom. Standing at the urinal, I overheard a
few guys asking, "Did you see those chicks? Who the hell is that

guy?" I chuckled to myself, "Someone they wish they could be." That night anyway.

In the month following our return, American Freezer, Inc.(AFI) continued to function under the direction of Danny and Allen Coulter, our service manager. They had also endured a barrage of media inquiries and non-stop calls from business friends and well wishers. Danny and Al were forced to set aside the business of running AFI. They manned the phones and dubbed it "Media Week."

I did return to the office shortly thereafter and found it difficult to concentrate on the business at hand. I had grown weary of the battle. In business, whether selling apples or airplanes, the problems remain essentially the same. There exists a daily struggle to increase revenues by reducing costs and increasing market share. To that, add the complexity of keeping everyone in the stream of commerce happy and, like the plague, the matter of avoiding the other guy's lawyer.

I didn't have the fight in me. I was exhausted and could not bring myself to action. It would be years before I slept well enough to have a good night's sleep. I did not have the energy or desire to continue the fight. AFI had proven to be a good business over the many years it had operated under my stewardship, and it provided a satisfactory income. Much to my chagrin, it had never performed in auto-pilot. I had hoped to groom a successor, or at the very least, a key employee imbued with the qualities essential to assuming control. At that time, Danny had not matured to the point where he could see the potential or for that matter, guide the company into the future. Undeniably charismatic, Danny, in time, would have done well with the company. Unfortunately, the timing was off. His interests, although not clearly defined at the time, lay elsewhere. To his credit, and my delight, he has since found his way and is quite successful.

Six months after returning from Mexico, and with alternating moods of relief and at times, a heavy heart, I shut down American Freezer, Inc. Under my ownership since 1977, the company had run continuously since 1946. In the summer of 1994, I set about the business of selling off its inventory, fixtures, trucks, and anything of value. Whenever I question the wisdom of closing the company Liz reminds me of the long hours and the pressure of running the company. She is absolutely right.

The telephone and mail brought something new every day in the months following our return. At home we were inundated with requests for interviews. We also received get-well cards from well intentioned strangers across the country and some letters from whackos. One such letter was typewritten on a postcard with no hint of its origin. It was beautiful. The following is a verbatim and precise typographical re-print of that letter. In fairness, I should add that most of the letters were written from the heart and accepted gratefully, but the wackos were much more fun.

To wit:

Mr. Chimenti,Presdident American Freezers Inc.,(address)

"As a taxpayer who paid for your rescue, I'd like to say you are a stupid s...Going out on a ski do in a foreign land like that. They are not as stupid as the Americans who go out and rescue (at great cost to the taxpayer) some a..h... who goe's out to ski although there are avalanche warnings out, goe's out into the ocean when he has no brains, no gas and can't swim probobly, and we the taxpayer pay for those damn rescues. Well since you own a freezer Co and had enough money to go to Mexico, you should pay the government back. In fact they should pass a bill that would make you guys pay back the government for use and pulling men away from their jobs in the coast guard, national guard, or woodsmen or park rangers, I am sick of reading about you idiots...keep the hell in your own back yard from now on or go somewhere and horse around with your own rescue people or bodyguards"

I love that guy. What a character. Also a coward. I wish I knew who he was, so I could have slapped him.

At the office we were treated to a major upswing in the number of resume's and job applications, sob stories and all. Located at the end of a dead end street in an industrial subdivision, and engaged in a business not readily visible to the general public, we were not accustomed to receiving many job requests. I sincerely admired their perseverance and responded to many of them. I wish I could have rewarded them all with a job.

Unlike myself, Liz didn't need to be schmoozed by the press and found no joy in dealing with reporters. Being of sound mind and possessing an unshakable sense of self-worth, Liz found them to be, with some exceptions, contemptible. I knew it would go away very soon and never come back. She wanted the media to go away. She was worried that our children would be at risk if people discovered where we lived. Footage of the front of our home was outlawed.

Of course, there were some inquiries which Liz was thrilled to consider. Not the least of which was a telephone call from a Michigan author by the name of Lowell Cauffiel who expressed an interest in writing a screenplay for a telefilm, a made for TV movie. Lowell's initial phone call to my office was met with indifference. So many calls were coming in that it was impossible to separate the good from the bad. I vaguely recognized Lowell's name, but did not bother to call him back. It did not interest me, initially, that he was interested in speaking to me because I had already been signed by an agent in Hollywood.

The decision to retain an agent had its origin in a conversation between myself, Liz, Dean Bruza our attorney and the Rubins, Stu and Andrea, a few weeks earlier. It was beyond the realm of belief that we would ever need representation in the form of an agent in the entertainment/movie business, but there we were; discussing intellectual property rights and the economic value of my life story. No longer willing to discuss our story with just anyone, Liz and I were advised to keep our mouths shut. With all the outside interest, Andrea offered to call her brother Sam and seek his guidance.

Andrea's brother Sam is the well renowned Director Sam Raimi. Andrea called her brother on my behalf. Talk about being fortuitous. I shook my head in goofy disbelief that I could have such incredible luck in the form of assistance from a powerful Hollywood director. The problem with Andrea's call was that Sam was in the middle of the desert filming "The Quick and the Dead" with Sharon Stone and Gene Hackman. They were all living out of trailers and working 20 hours a day. According to Andrea, Sam called home to California late in the evening everyday. Late in the evening on the west coast meant the middle of the night for us. She would attempt to reach him then. The sweetheart that she is, Andrea stayed up late and discussed the matter with him. Sam recommended that we speak with his agent at International Creative Management (ICM), the biggest talent agency in Hollywood. He then paved the way for us. Without his help we would have been left to the wolves for the entertainment industry is not for the weak of heart. They really do eat their young. We were extremely fortunate to have been sponsored, in a loosely held way, by Sam Raimi. Hollywood is all about power, and Andrea's brother has his share. During our negotiations with ICM, I was never under the illusion that my story meant anything to the people involved in the process of getting our movie sold. We had made a splash with all the television and print coverage, but we were very small fish indeed. They were all business and very cold. At the conclusion of a conversation with ICM, I did not return the receiver to its cradle feeling warm and fuzzy. Initially, it was getting done because ICM was asked to get it done. Period. My agent was Julie Weitz, a no-nonsense, here's the way it is, here's how much it's worth, here's the deal, kind of woman. I was very excited.

Julie explained the process of getting a movie made. Typically, it takes 9-18 months to get a movie into production. Therefore, we would sign an option for a period of one year with any production company that expressed an interest in our story. We would be paid for the option at the time of the execution of that option. The first step was to sign an exclusive representation contract with ICM to handle my 'exclusive life rights' and this 'package' as it pertained to the event. ICM would work under a 'package fee.' The Chimenti family would not pay a fee or percentage to anyone. If the 'package' was sold to a production company, ICM's fee would be paid under the movie production budget. Julie explained that ICM would package our story by hiring a screenwriter to meet with me, write the screenplay, and hire the actors to play our roles. It was her opinion that our story would be a 2 hour telefilm; what we commonly refer to as a 'made for TV' movie. It would most likely be a Sunday night movie. The only problem with our story was that it would be difficult to dramatize. "Floating," according to Julie "does not make a story." The downside was that I was alone in the ocean with no dialogue. If she only knew.

If sold, the money for the option period was okay. The money for the movie, if it were made, was terrific. Not enough for anyone to retire on, but very very nice. There were well established parameters for the amount of money our story could command. I complained about the lower number; she agreed to do her best. Unlike the option period, full payment for the movie would be forthcoming only upon the start of principal photography.

International Creative Management, according to Julie, had a strong literary division for book sales. In that regard, she would make inquiries in New York as well.

We were so excited. A little vacation that turned into a night-mare, that turned into a movie.   `

We received fully executed originals of the contract between the Chimenti family and ICM.

We became officially, wards of the most powerful talent agency in the world, and I, for one, had no talent. Only in America. I should have tried my luck at the nearest crap table. I had a hot winning streak. I had not, as yet, called Lowell Cauffiel when Julie Weitz called to inform me that one of their clients, a writer, had expressed interest in the story of a guy lost at sea. It was his desire to write a treatment and produce the story. He called his agent. His agent was also my agent. His name was Lowell Cauffiel. It was time to call Lowell Cauffiel.

I invited Lowell to come to our home. Our visit, and numer-ous subsequent phone calls with Lowell, was very pleasant and informative. Lowell regaled us with stories of the 'real' Hollywood, a not so pleasant place. It was for that reason that Lowell eschewed the idiosyncrasies of Hollywood for a normal life in a small Michi-gan town.

Lowell began life as a respected writer for the Detroit News and had gone on to write a number of well received 'true life' books. Very dark, with perhaps his experience as a newspaper writer thrust-ing him into the underbelly of the human experience, his books were a narrative of violence and death. Lowell served as the Marlin Perkins of the human animal kingdom. His first book told the true story of Allen Canty, a successful Grosse Pointe, MI psychologist who was found murdered and chopped into pieces, his tortured remains scattered throughout the city. His second book, 'Masquerade,' documented the serial murders of the residents of a nursing home by a group of lesbian aides. "Masquerade" was also a true story that garnered national attention.

It was my impression that Lowell had been affected, in a not so pleasant way, by the investigation and telling of those stories.

Lowell created a treatment, the precursor to a screenplay, and effectively retired the problem of dialogue by concentrating on Liz's efforts to find me. Her story, on its own merits, made for exciting dramatic possibilities. He shipped it off to Julie at ICM and we were on our way. It was now up to our agents to sell the package.

Beyond selling our movie, there were few, if any, income generating opportunities.

We entertained many other inquiries from the media. Linda Henry, a writer for Readers Digest contacted us to inquire if she could do a story for a future issue. Magazines do not typically pay for their stories. It was no different in our case. Again, it made no difference to us. How could anyone, in their right mind, turn down an offer to be the subject of a major story in Readers Digest? Printed in 19 languages, Readers Digest has a readership in excess of 20 million. It didn't get bigger than that. We were overwhelmed with joy that we were candidates for a story in their magazine. Readers Digest picks their stories with a very watchful eye. It is not easy getting into their magazine.

Linda flew in with her newborn baby, checked into a local hotel, and came to our home throughout the weekend, gathering data for her article. She was very pleasant and wrote from the heart, for Linda was passionate about life, she herself the victim of a senseless tragedy. A number of years prior, Linda was involved in a car accident. Her child was killed and she suffered extensive injuries that left her partially disabled.

Our story did appear in the November 1995 issue and spanned six pages. An interesting footnote to the business of getting a story published, Readers Digest, in addition to the exacting story selection process, also conducted exhaustive historical research to corroborate all that was written in the body of the article. Leaving nothing to chance, the editors at Readers Digest made phone calls to all parties whose names appeared in the story. In our case, calls were made to Germany for confirmation by Captain Richter, as well as the owners of the shipping line and Liz and myself. In fact, the editors kept calling and calling checking this and that and everything. It really got very annoying. They took nothing at face value. According to Linda Henry, her article had been tweaked many times since her original submission.

Redbook magazine sent a writer and photographer and published an article. A women's magazine, Redbook was interested in Liz's achievements. They wanted to celebrate the story of a woman who had struggled to save her husbands life. To their credit, they didn't even talk to me. I was happy that Liz would be singled out for applause.

A producer from the 'Gabrielle' show called and asked if I would appear on their talk show. Gabrielle was a former cast member of Beverly Hills 90210 and had her own talk show. Scheduled to air in just a few days, they offered to fly me to Los Angeles, pick me up by limousine, pick up the tab for a hotel room and pay for all meals while in Los Angeles. I inquired if I would be paid for my appearance. To my best recollection they refused to pay.

They were doing a show on 'survivors.' In a weak moment I agreed to do the show, but insisted that they also pay for Liz to accompany me out to California. I did not want to go alone. The producer said that it was an unusual request but she would check and call me back. They called me back within 10 minutes and gave the green light.

...and then I got to thinking. I had been on an airplane before. I had been in a limousine. I was no stranger to a hotel room. I had even lived in Los Angeles when I was younger. A four hour trip there and another four hours back. What a pain. To top it off they would probably make me look like an idiot and they weren't even paying me.

I changed my mind.

Liz loved doing the dirty work. She called the show the next day and informed them that we would not be coming out. They were hot. Very hot. They had finalized plans for the show and were panicky. I felt bad. Liz set the phone down and said "Oh well. Too bad for them." Liz is sometimes great to watch in action.

I also received books in the mail. One such book was entitled 'Rescued' and written by Dave and Barb Anderson. The Andersons sent me their book with a personal note that drew a parallel to a similar event they had experienced. On the evening of August 13, 1993 their chartered missionary aviation plane crashed at 100 m.p.h. into the Bering Sea, 22 miles southwest of

Nome, Alaska. The water temperature was a bone numbing 37 degrees. There is no record of anyone surviving a plane crash into the Bering Sea. They were the first. Dedicated to Jesus Christ, they published their book, recorded video tapes, and spread the word of their miracle.

One of the most satisfying aspects of the aftermath at sea were the countless letters and artwork I received from schoolchildren. In one particular case, a teacher had shared one of the articles describing my story with his class. The children decided to write to me. He collected all the letters and pictures drawn by the students and stuffed them into a large manila envelope with a cover letter that described his reason for reading my story to his students. He was dedicated to teaching the children to "appreciate life, family, and friends, and that we are all special people. (My) story of courage and will to survive exemplified this point." He concluded his letter with the hope that I would write to them.

Their letters were written with enthusiasm, filled with questions, and contained their sincerest hopes for my recovery. I couldn't ignore those children. My first idea, and the most reasonably expedient, was to write one letter addressed to all the children thanking them for their letters and wonderful artwork and answer a few of their general questions. The subject of sharks was a prevailing fascination for all the children in their letters, so that was easy. I decided that one letter was not good enough. I imagined the innocent face of each child opening a personal letter from me and couldn't resist writing to each of them individually.

There were over 30 children in that class. It took me a long time to get it all done. A significant investment in time, I finally wrapped up a personal letter to each individual student and sent it off to their teacher. They were so filled with exuberance over my having written back to them that they decided to send me another letter! As before, I received a large packet with over 30 more letters. I couldn't do it again. I did write one final letter to the teacher and signed off. It was a very satisfying experience. I was proud of myself. In preceding years, I would have had my longtime secretary, Scottie, read one or two letters to herself and let her respond in my name, if she were so inclined.

Another producer called. This time it was a producer for J.P. McCarthy, one of the most respected radio personalities in Michigan. With a national reputation, J.P. McCarthy, to my father's generation, was a god unto himself. J.P. wanted to do a 'live' interview with me. I was so thoroughly tired of doing interviews. I didn't want ANY MORE INTERVIEWS.

But, J.P. McCarthy was my dad's personal favorite. For my father, I could not refuse this accomodation. Not given to outward displays of enthusiasm, I knew that my father would, nonetheless, have a puff in his chest if his son was on J.P.'s radio show. He wouldn't jump for joy on the outside, but I knew he would overflow with quiet pride in his son. The interview was arranged for the next morning at a predesignated time. Purposely casual, a 'no big deal' tone in my voice, but laughing inside, I informed my dad that I would be on the J.P. McCarthy show in the morning. My father was in his car on the way to work when the show came on the air. As J.P. was wrapping up our interview, I fed him an amusing anecdote that I knew he would appreciate. I said, "J.P., I thought you might like to know that I sleep on a water bed." He roared with laughter and wrapped up the interview.

My father called to tell me how proud of me he was. A gift to my father.

Apparently, someone from Ripleys Believe It Or Not caught wind of my story and saw fit to include me in their catalog of notable events. A drawing and short caption was published in the comic section of every newspaper in the country.

The interest and accolades kept coming and coming. I did absolutely nothing to garner any attention or give life to the story of my struggle at sea. Articles continued to appear in various publications over an extended period of time. Even rags, such as the Sun, printed articles; right alongside articles of JFK's re-incarnation and Elvis coming back to life. Real schlock, replete with references to "Dazed Dale" and "Lucky Dale being saved!! by a coke bottle as curious fish would come up for a nibble at his arms and legs."

Liz and I were also invited to be guests of the Red Cross at their very exclusive annual 'Gala in Red' dinner, a major fund raiser for Red Cross Emergency Services in southeastern Michigan. I was to be singled out as their special guest during the welcoming ceremonies. Moderated by TV personality Rich Fisher, the Gala in Red event was graced with none other than Elizabeth Dole, then head of the American Red Cross. Liz and I had the opportunity to speak with Mrs. Dole. A remarkable woman, we were more than anxious to meet her. We couldn't understand how she could be married to Bob, that cantankerous old bastard.

The room was filled with a who's who of the rich and powerful. I found myself seated next to Heinz and Wally Prechter. Heinz
is a major industrialist and the founder of AMS Sunroof.

At the conclusion of our meal, Rich Fisher took to the microphone to introduce the night's special guests. I was asked to
stand and be recognized. I was illuminated by a large spotlight
that swept the room. I stood to the applause and with a small
movement of my hand and a slight nod, gratefully thanked the
crowd. I was thankful that it was done and over with. I was even
more pleased that I had made Liz happy. She was the most beautiful woman in the room and she was very proud of me. For that I
was very thankful.

I was also annoyed with Rich Fisher. He had mispronounced
my last name. Actually, I had a few drinks and was looking for
some trouble. I asked myself, "How could an anchorman mispro-
nounce a simple, phonetic name?"

I would have a few words with him.

I caught him in the bathroom talking to Richard Kughn,
the owner of Lionel Trains, another rich industrialist, and two
older men, both smelling of very old money. I decided to roast
Rich right then and there. I ignored the fact that they were engaged in a conversation and with feigned indignation, stepped
between Rich Fisher and the other men. Pointing my finger at
him, I began to chastise him. I opened by saying "My wife is very
unhappy with you." I repeated myself. "My wife is very unhappy
with you." "She is standing just outside that door and she is VERY

unhappy." Lowering my voice, leaning in, and with a New York Italian accent, I suggested "When she is unhappy, I am unhappy." I then shut up and awaited his reaction.

Rich was beside himself. Flapping his jaw in disbelief, confounded by my diatribe, he was speechless. "What? What? Why is she unhappy with me?"

I said, "Rich," with the tone of one scolding a child, "Rich, you mispronounced my last name and my last name is also her last name. She is very unhappy about that and she is going to have a few words with you when you leave this bathroom. I just wanted to let you know. I feel sorry for you."

Silence. Complete silence, I savored the moment, kept a pulse on the timing and on cue, delivered a grin as wide as a house. I never saw a funnier moment. I let him off the hook and he laughed like a hyena. Rich Fisher, Dick Kughn and I left the bathroom like old war buddies. Liz really was nearby as was Rich's wife. Introductions were made all around.

Other than the appearance of Tom Schoenith, of Roostertail fame, who sidled up next to me and proceeded to remind me that I was a mere interloper, and that my pumpkin would appear at midnight, it was a great evening.

In the ensuing years, Liz endeared herself to the movers and shakers in the community of Red Cross volunteers and for a time, became a valued member of their organization. Most of the women who contributed their time to the Red Cross were the wives of very rich men, and whose time was their own. To her dismay, the restraint of full time employment has prevented Liz from maintaining an active role as a volunteer in the service of the Red Cross.

I was asked by many schools to give motivational talks and decided to accept the invitation of a few schools, including a graduate class at the University of Michigan and a number of grade schools. I was quite comfortable speaking to large groups and had delivered many lectures to a variety of groups during my years in business. Emotionally, it was another matter. Reliving the experience, at a time so near the actual episode, brought tears and exhaustion.

My life had turned into a major highway with countless lanes going in all directions at the same time, and with no specificity of purpose; and that was okay. It was a fun ride.

In keeping with my newfound role as 'man of the moment,' we received a phone call from Julie at ICM with the astounding news that she had sold our story. We jumped for joy.

Paragon Entertainment Corporation, a large company with corporate offices in Los Angeles, Toronto, and Vancouver had agreed to an Option Agreement for the "Life Story Rights/ Chimenti Family" for a period of one(1) year. With a green light from ICM our agents, and forwarded from the law firm representing Paragon Entertainment Corporation, we were sent a contract confirming our agreement.

Considered a 'standard' contract, the subject agreement spelled out the conditions ceding all control of our story to Paragon, when and how much we would be paid, and our role in supporting the movie production. It included language that called for a bonus payable upon "(i) our signature of an agreement for distribution of the Picture outside of the United States and Canada and our receipt of an advance pursuant to such agreement." It also included language that required the Chimenti family to "use our best efforts in coordinating the date of initial publication of any literary work based upon the 'story' in conjunction with the initial exhibition of the Picture."..and on and on.

ICM encouraged us to sign it and return to them for ratification as soon as possible. Tempted to hurry it along, and worried that a dark cloud might pass over in the time it took to reach their offices, my initial intent was to have Liz and the children sign it and send it back immediately. Fortunately, my years in business had bred a modicum of cynicism for I am trusting by nature and skeptical by experience. I had the good sense to slow down and run it by my lawyer. Indeed, Dean, our lawyer, found a number of glaring deficiencies. One such problem existed in the form of a contractual requirement to act as a consultant during filming. I was thrilled over the prospect of going 'on location.' What could be finer?

However, Dean pointed out that a provision for payment of expenses was conspicuously absent. It had never crossed my mind. It suddenly occurred to me that it could get expensive. Very expensive. It was entirely possible that filming could take place in Mexico or some exotic locale and that my services might be required for an extended period of time, most assuredly at the whim of the director, and just as certainly without regard to cost. Filming could easily take a month or more.

"A standard contract? They have got to be kidding." Welcome to the world of entertainment. It was intuitively obvious, with the benefit of my lawyers' hindsight, that the absence of language which would have provided for my expenses was their intent. They had too many lawyers and too many sharpshooter accountants for the issue of expenses to have been left out accidentally. Real nice guys. My pals.

We were the beneficiaries of the resolution of that difference of opinion in the form of language drafted by our attorney that provided me with expenses for air transportation, accommodations, and "reasonably necessary" living expenses.

They sent us a check.

Over a period of one year, the option period, we kept a fairly constant vigil on the status of Paragon's interest. We wanted to keep up the momentum and therefore applied subtle pressure through our agent. But, we did not want to become a source of irritation in the process. ICM had many more important clients. Liz and I always felt like the neophytes we truly were. To his credit, Lowell Cauffiel always made himself available and kept us posted. The coincidental circumstance of our having the same agent worked to our benefit because Lowell was a day to day client of ICM and was 'in the loop,' so to speak. Lowell explained that ICM's role went beyond selling the idea to Paragon Entertainment. Their fee, which Julie Weitz had explained earlier, required them to deliver an entire 'package' to the production company. In our case, ICM was obligated to have the screenplay written, hire the actors, and deliver the package to Paragon Entertainment Corporation.

Ultimately, the movie did not get made and our contract with Paragon Entertainment expired. Not before a number of exciting possibilities appeared before us, however. Either Julie at ICM, or more likely, Lowell, informed us that Lindsay Wagner, the former "Bionic Woman" had a 5 picture deal with CBS. Apparently, Lindsay Wagner was tied in with a writer who wanted the deal to satisfy, in part, his obligation to CBS. Lindsay Wagner would portray Liz in the movie. I assumed they could not find anyone handsome enough to play me.

The business of getting movies produced revolves more upon what some brash 23 year old producer had for breakfast, than a business teeming with individuals dedicated to clear and rational thinking. It's either alive or it's dead, or it's alive again...

We were more than satisfied that we were allowed to dream for a moment. Another dimension to a very interesting life.

As referenced earlier in this writing, each new article brought a rash of cards and letters from across the country. I have crossed the path of many people, some of whom, I am pleased to note, have enriched my life.

One such person came to me in the form of a telephone call shortly after the Readers Digest article appeared. How she got through to us I will never know, but somehow, the caller acquired my Aunt Lina's telephone number. My Aunt gave her our home number. That could have been dangerous and I was, at first, concerned. It took only a moment to recognize that my Aunt exercised laudable judgement, for the woman, Yvonne Zubi, was in a profound state of depression. Yvonne's daughter, Christina, had perished on a jet-ski, with her companion, in the Atlantic Ocean off the coast of Long Island, New York. Inconsolable, Yvonne had read the article in Readers Digest and set her mind to the task of finding me. My initial reaction to Yvonne's call was one of suppressed annoyance. This woman, a complete stranger from California, had invaded my personal space with the intention of forming some grassroots movement to foist awareness of the dangers of jet-ski's upon the American people. Yvonne felt that my celebrity status would lend credibility to that effort. I had absolutely no interest in becoming involved. It occurred to me during the course of our conversation, that Yvonne was not some crazy person. In fact, she struck me as a very bright, well educated woman who was in a great deal of pain; who really didn't have an agenda. She wanted to be heard. I represented one who had experienced Christina's pain. I had lived through the terror that Christina must have endured. I had experienced thirst and exhaustion and hopelessness. Yvonne wanted to touch her daughter through me.

We spent two hours on the telephone that evening. I explained my experience with the process of dying to Yvonne. I felt more than qualified to do so. I explained to her that, at the moment of her death, Christina felt no pain, no remorse, no guilt, no terror. She passed effortlessly, a peaceful introduction to the energy of the universe. Yvonne trusted that my words rang true. In some small way I had contributed to her own rehabilitation.

Yvonne and I have never met each other in person, yet consider ourselves good friends, and mutually the richer for it. She is an incredible person. Frankly, I consider myself the 'poor cousin' in our relationship, not in the literal definition of 'poor,' but more appropriately, in the passionate spiritual awareness that Yvonne has weaved into her daily life, and which I choose to generally ignore. It has never been my practice to embrace a religious or spiritual perspective as a benchmark for my daily conduct. Capable of understanding the moral complexities of a spiritual life, and smart enough not to disavow its existence, I choose to live a much simpler life.

Of all the chance events that occurred, none was more serendipitous than meeting an individual by the name of Joe Rudzinski. Joe was a member of the same health club to which I belonged. I had never met him before the day he walked up to me, introduced himself, and offered his sincerest congratulations. Joe also explained that he was the son-in-law of Chuck Muer, the same Chuck Muer who had perished at sea with his wife and two friends. He pointed out that his wife was Chuck's daughter. The same daughter who had moved mountains in search of her mother and father. The same daughter who would never see her parents again. I was aghast that I had come face to face with a direct link to the very people whose fate I had contemplated at great length during my struggle at sea. I felt an immediate sense of guilt. Here was a man whose family had endured untold grief—and he was genuinely happy for me. I survived and they did not. As mentioned earlier in this writing, I had measured the chances of my survival against the odds the Muer's had faced and the knowledge that they had surely died at sea. I am humbled and indebted to Joe for his kindness. Having battled the same beast and lived, I hope through this writing, to share some insight into the last moments of the lives of Mr. and Mrs. Muer, with their survivors. Perhaps my wishes in that regard are inappropriate and presumptuous. Perhaps old wounds are better left undisturbed. As I swam alone in the middle of the ocean, most assuredly at deaths' door, the Muers were a source of strength, their fate a standard which I vowed to change. I benefitted from their misfortune. They had, in abstentia, given me strength.

A short time after returning from Mexico, Liz and I filed a lawsuit in the amount of 14 million dollars. Our attorney, Dennis O'Bryan, to whom we are indebted, and who has our deepest respect, and affection, called a press conference to announce the filing of that action. The reaction to the announcement of our intention to seek damages against the Hotel and the tour company was enormous. All the local newspapers ran articles in their OP(opinion) sections denouncing our decision to file a lawsuit. Particularly venomous, many of the columnists decided that I should consider myself "grateful for another chance at life." Indeed I was. I was also very hurt by their hostile words. Dennis responded and was given equal space in a subsequent article to rebut. He wrote in part, "I have for years represented people who have gone on foreign vacations, and frankly, am sick and tired of having them come back injured, maimed, disfigured, or dead, with no avenue of recourse." In our hearts, we believe in the righteousness of our decision. As of this writing, our complaints remain unresolved.

E P I L O G U E

In the restaurants, the locker room, the street, talk of business; people engaged in the stream of commerce, spirited discussions about selling this or that, marketing departments, managers, products, seminars, —all the things I now find odd; everyone involved on a daily basis with those things I no longer understand, people convinced of the significance of their work, whose view of the world is shaped entirely by their work, and whose entire consciousness is dictated by that work. I am jealous because I do not understand how to re-engage myself into the daily machinations of the human experience. I look askew at the idea of expending energy on the 'insignificant details' of the human experience, what I refer to as a fundamentally meaningless pre-occupation with nonsense. I struggle, instead, with the matter of death, an equally meaningless pre-occupation. It is unshakable.

It has been suggested that the process of writing this memoir would provide me with a necessary 'catharsis' in order for me to exorcise the demons within. Catharsis? The word alone annoys the hell out me. I don't believe in catharsis. To postulate that re-visiting an 'event' will somehow reveal a hidden 'psychological truth,' or precipitate a metamorphosis of the spirit is nonsense.

Has my life changed as a result of this incredible experience? Of course. To define that change as 'unfortunate' and therefore distinct from the normal human experience? I do not know. The truth is that it will not let me go. A trip to the mailbox in the front of my home conjures up thoughts of survival. A cold wind passes over me and my thoughts shift to ideas on how to survive the cold if I can't get back to my house. I am drawn to examine the chances of survival given the temperature, the windspeed, how long I might be subject to the prevailing temperatures. How might I best utilize the newspaper in the mailbox as a source of warmth? With sleep out of the question, how long could I keep moving in order to maintain proper core body temperature?

Being lost in the ocean was the defining moment in my life. It is the filter through which I see the world, the filter through which I conduct my life. It was the gateway to the abyss from which I judge all situations.

This writing a catharsis? I think not. Rather, a reminder that I am really alive. These are the only stimuli to which I respond. There is little else that awakens my emotions more than revisiting this experience. This writing allows me to feel the same emotional touchstones over and over. It is a very powerful stimulus.

Other than the opportunity to provide love and guidance to my children and the same love and companionship to my wife, whom I adore, I struggle to find a concrete meaning for my personal existence. The question of 'when' I will return to the moment of my death occupies the forefront of my attention. I am not afraid. It was a nice place.

I am a young man, however, and trust that with the help of my wife, and many friends, I will find my way here on earth. This is a nice place too. I have a good life. I am thankful for all that I have.

A   H O R S E   N A M E D
N E V E R   D E S P A I R

I am reminded of an event that transpired on a cold winter day, a few seasons past. Liz and I were alone in my office, at peace with the world, busy wallpapering and painting, music playing quietly in the background. Occupied with the business of putting paint to brush, my mind idle to the world, I was suddenly drawn to a mixture of tears and pride. Over the radio, we heard the voice of Mort Crim, a former television anchorman and now nationally syndicated radio columnist. He was speaking about me.

He had some "Second Thoughts" to share with his listeners. Later reprinted in his book*, it went as follows:

Stubborness can be irritating.

It can also be life saving

I recall leading a newscast one evening with the story of a very stubborn man. His jet-ski had stopped running, and he was too far from shore for anyone to see or hear him.

The sun baked his skin as currents carried him farther and

---

* *Second Thoughts,* Mort Crim, ©1997 Mort Crim Communications, Inc., Publisher: Health Communications, Inc.

farther out to sea.

Finally he could no longer see land, and for nearly three days and nights he drifted.

But he never gave up. He hung on, stubbornly, and eventually was spotted by the crew of a ship and rescued.

What if he had given up just one hour before help arrived?

Fortunately, it wasn't this man's nature to quit. And so he hung on.

How many entrepreneurs have succeeded simply because they hung in there a little longer after everyone was telling them it was no use? No matter how tough it was, they were too stubborn to let despair take over.

A woman in lower Manhattan was a soft touch for anyone down on his luck. One morning she took pity on the man she'd seen standing on a corner near her apartment. He looked so forlorn, and she wanted to encourage him.

Pressing a dollar into his hand, she whispered, "Never Despair."

Next day as she passed him, the man stopped the woman and handed her nine dollars.

"What's this?" she asked.

"It's your winnings," the man responded.

Yes, you guessed it. The object of this woman's charity was a bookie, and a horse named Never Despair had won at 8-1.

In the great race of life it's an even better bet that Never Despair will always finish in the money.

I am proud to have never despaired.

Made in the USA
Monee, IL
02 July 2020

34299327R00098